Lake Monsters and Odd Creatures of the Great Lakes.

By Shetan Noir

Shetan Noir publications

Copyright © 2018, by Shetan Noir

Publisher: Shetan Noir

Brighton, Michigan
Author, Illustrator, Layout artist, Copy editor,
Image editor: Shetan Noir

Table of Contents

Acknowledgments

To my family and friends, research assistants
Thank you

Introduction

There is always something to explore as long as you let your curiosity lead you. New discoveries of the ancient fossil records are made every week and new species are found constantly.
  The world is filled with anomalies and mysteries yet to be solved.
Since early humans first traveled the great lakes in makeshift canoes and rafts. A spoken tradition of telling reports of Lake monsters began. From the mighty Mishipeshu, The great water Lynx to possible land locked whales species. Native Americans were seeing creatures in the great lakes long before European settlers brought their own folktales and myths to these lands.
  The Lake monsters ranged in forms from serpentine to turtle shaped. Other creatures are described as an Amalgamation of different parts of several species.
Some creature sightings of more recent times include reports of bull sharks and crocodilian species living in the great lakes. Giant horned snakes and freshwater octopus/squids have also been claimed for attacks.

Many of the monster sightings came from boat captains and boat passengers crossing the great lakes. Theses reports came long before P.T. Barnum styled publicity stunts and small towns wanting tourist dollars.

 These sightings were often reported to the local court magistrates and harbor authorities. The statements given by witnesses were normally published in the local newspapers and these witnesses were pushed into the public's eye. Making them available to criticism or praise depending on the readers.
 So what have people been seeing all these years in the waters of the Great lakes and in the land-locked lakes of each Great lakes state.
 Are these real living, breathing creatures? Are they from the realm of the paranormal? Interdimensional creatures travel from one time and space to another? Are they just myth, folktale and legends? Hoax's?
We may never know. None of these creatures have ever been caught and examined by the scientific community. Physical evidence at best is blurred pictures and video.
Yet the sighting reports date back to the 1700's and people still make claims of odd sightings and experiences on the Great lakes.
 This book covers many aspects of the Lake monster phenomenon
 from the fossil records to Native American legends to possible real misplaced creatures.
The photographs and drawings are in the book to help give a reference point. The drawings are based on the actual description of each creature and my own interpretation of what those creature's may have looked like.

Real Monsters

Chapter one

The great lakes

The great lakes consist of Huron, Ontario, Michigan, Erie and Superior. The acronym Homes can be used to remember the names. These great lakes or inland seas hold the greatest amount of fresh water in the world. Over 6 quadrillion gallons and covering over 95,160 square miles or 246,463 square kilometers. That makes the combined mass larger than the State of Texas.

That is a lot of water for living space, no matter what size species or creatures swim in it. Currently there are 3,500 known species of plants and animals living in the great lakes. Not to mention over 170 different fish species both native and non-native.

Lake Huron was named Karegnondi after the Wyandot tribe and the Huron tribe that lived in the area. Lake Huron is the second largest great lake by surface area. 23,000 square miles/59,600 square kilometers. It has the longest shoreline at 3,827 mile/ 6,157 kilometers. It has a water volume of 850 cubic miles/3,543 cubic kilometers. Lake Huron has an average depth of 32 fathoms or 195 ft deep. Its deepest point is 125 fathoms

deep or 750 ft.
It has a length of 206 statute miles/332 kilometers. It has a breath of 183 statute miles/295 kilometers.

Lake Ontario, The lake of shining water as named by the Huron tribe. It is the smallest of the great lakes with a measured surface area of 7,340 square miles/18,960 square kilometers. It is much deeper that Lake Erie and can hold 4 times more water, an estimate of 393 cubic miles/1,640 cubic kilometers more water. Lake Ontario has an average depth of 47 fathoms or 283ft. It has a maximum depth is 133 fathoms or 802 ft.

Lake Michigan, The Ojibwas called this lake Michigami meaning Large lake. It is the 3rd largest great lake with a surface area of 22,300 square miles/57,800 square kilometers. It has an average depth of 46 fathoms or 279 ft. and a maximum depth of 153 fathoms or 923 ft.
It is actually attached to Lake Huron and could be considered one lake. Lake Michigan has an unusual tide pattern with a slow moving circular pattern that is like a Cul-de-sac formation.

Lake Erie or Erielhonan as the Iroquoian called it. The word meant Long tail and was a good description of the lake's shape. Erie is the 4th largest great lake with a surface area of 9,910 square miles/25,700 square kilometers. It has the smallest volume of water at 116 cubic miles. 484 cubic kilometers. It has an average depth of 10 fathoms or 62 ft. and a maximum depth of 35 fathoms or 210 ft. Lake Erie is the warmest great lake because of it's shallow depths.

Lake Superior, The great inland sea named Gitche Gumee. It is the largest great lake with a surface area of 31,699 square miles/ 82,100 cubic kilometers and water volume of 2,903 cubic miles/12,100 cubic kilometers.

Chapter two

Formation of the Great lakes

The five Great lakes were formed during the ice ages. At one time great marine reptiles, fish and mammals swam in their depths. The great lakes region was underwater for much of the Paleozoic era and many on the species living there were water bound. During the Cambrian era, Michigan started forming into it's mitten like shape and the land mass was then located near the Equator.

During the Ordovicain period, Michigan did have large patches of water that were devoid of any land living species. This gave primitive species like trilobites and cone shaped cephalopods a change to thrive.

The Silurian period show that warm shallow seas flowed down from the Arctic. The great lakes had a subtropical climate that aided in the development of vast coral reefs. The remains of which are found in treasures pieces of Petoskey stones.

The largest and oldest of these reefs were formed in the the upper peninsula of Michigan and Wisconsin.

Once these subtropical seas retreated, a fossil rich desert was left. This then became limestone and formed the landscape of today.

The Devonian period saw both salt and fresh water seas 400 million years ago near the great lakes. These waters were filled with armor plates fish species that are relatives to the great lakes Gar, pike and Sturgeon.
350 million years ago, The Carboniferous period saw insects and ferns claiming the lands of the great lakes. A sub-period called the Mississippian saw a new sea coming and going across the land. Changing the landscape every time it did. At the Carboniferous periods end, The Pennsylvanian sub-period. Michigan became a semi-tropical jungle.
   The next 300 million years was the Permian period. This time period is a bit of a mystery. All 3 periods of the Mesozoic levels are missing. Having been wiped from history as the land masses becomes the supercontinent Pangea. The Triassic and Jurassic periods saw dinosaurs roaming the lands.
   The movements of the land masses were not beneficial to the preservation of fossils. The landmasses known as the great lakes states made a slow journey northward to their current place on the map. During that time the creatures living in the waters and on the land changed, adapted and evolved. Most of the great lakes area fossil records were lost to history and have been impossible to recover. There may never be a complete record of what lived in the Great lakes.
   The ice sheets that moved across the great lakes area were estimated to have had an average thickness of 1.25 miles to 2 mile These ice sheets were capable of moving megablocks of bedrock that weighed millions of tons and measured sometime 3 miles. These megablocks were moved more that 200 miles or more.
   This helped to carve out the great lakes and other land formations such as valleys, kettles and ridges.

   The fossil records that are known of the great lakes hold an interesting array of fish species and odd creatures. Ranging in size from a few inches to several feet. For the purpose of this book I will be looking at fish and creatures of size.

Pike
Esocidae family

The Northern Pike 20 – 30 ft long, 1-2 lbs
The Muskellunge 6ft long, 30 – 40 lbs

Salmonidae family

Lake Trout 3 feet, 50 lbs estimated

Gadidae Family

Burbot

Ictaluridae family

Channel Catfish 50 inch, 30lbs

Sciaenidae family

Freshwater drum 2ft., 25-30 lbs.

Cyclopteridae family

Lumpfin 2ft., 13Lbs.

Dunkleosteidae family Placodermi fish

Dunkleosteus terrelli – 20- 33 ft, 1 ton found in Cleveland shale formations, Rock river, OH. Lived 360 million years ago. Had up 8000 lbs pf pressure per inch in its jaws. Dunkleosteus ate the sharks species of it's time.

The armor plated head of the Dunkleosteus

Protitanichthys Rockportensis 7 ft 4in, Found in Rockland State park, Michigan

Protitanichthys Fossatus 20 centimeters/7.9 inches

Coccosteua 40 centimeters, 16inches.

Cladoselache family (Shark)
Most found in Cleveland shale formation Cleveland, Ohio

Illustration 1: Edestus Giganteus (Giant scissor-toothed shark) S. Illinois

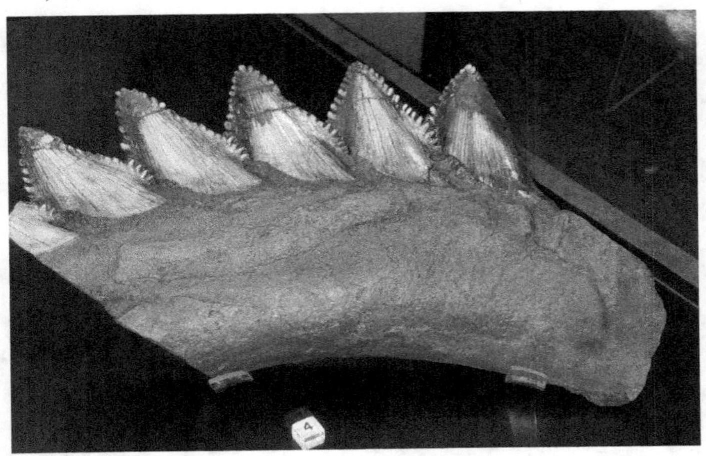

Cladoselache 1.8 meters/5.9 ft in length

Diademodus hydei (shark) 40 centimeters in length

Stethacanthus (shark) 70 centimeters in length

Ctenacanthus 50 centimeters in length

Orodus 2 meters/7 ft. in length

Acanthodians (spiny shark)

Ageleodus Pectinatus

Glikmanius occidentalis

Celphalopods

Huronia

Chouteauoceras

Maccoyoceras

Pseudorthocerua

Tornoceras-

Whales

toothed whales
White whales (Delphinapterus Leucas) 3,000 lbs found near the
Champlain Sea (late wisconsinan). Complete skeleton found
 near Cornwall, Ontario
Sperm whales- one lumbar vertebrate and two ribs were found
 in a Michigan swamp near Lenawee County.

Baleen whales

Rorquals- (Megaptera Novaeangliae) 32,000 lbs found in the great lakes area, From the Pleistocene era.

Humpback Whales- 60,000 lbs Found near Welsh gravel pit near Smiths falls, Lanark County, Ontario

Bowhead Whales and Right Whales

Bowhead whale (Balaena Mysticetus) – 140,000 lbs Found near Hanson's gravel pit near White lake, Ontario. A single rib was found during a cellar excavation in Genesee County.

Finback Whale- a single large rib was found in Oscoda Michigan

Mosasaurs fossils found by native American tribes of the Midwest. The tribes drew images of the Mosasaurs. These may have most likely been Leurospondylus, a fresh water plesiosaur,

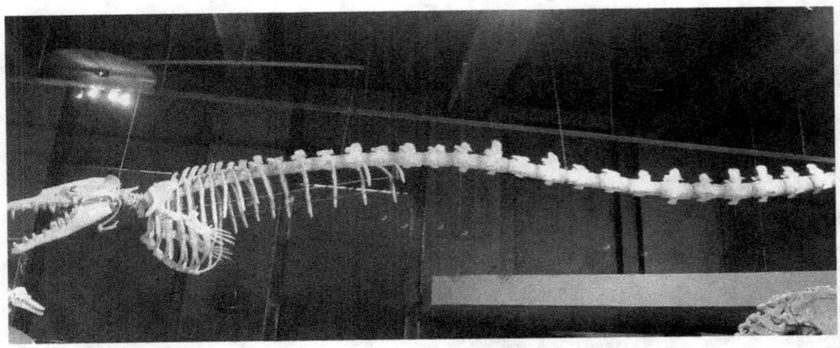

Rutiodon- The wrinkled tooth Triassic Phytosaur, a distant relative of the crocodile. Measuring 8 ft. long and 300lbs.

Fexedia Striegeli – a carnivorious Temnospondyl. It lived near the Pittsburgh area 300 million years ago. Looking somewhat like a salamander it was estimated to be 2 ft. long.

Hynerpeton was a carnivorous Tetrapod. Living in the late Devonian period. This first true Amphibian was very similar to the lobe finned fish. Fossil were found near Red hill, Pennsylvania.

Chapter Three

**Modern Aquatic species of the Great Lakes,
 Both Native and Non-native**

Seaweed and Aquatic plants(growing over 12 inches in
 length)

Water Milfoil- 2 meters
Water weed- 3 meters
Curly pond weed- 2 meters
Wild celery- 3 ft
Smart weeds- 4 ft
Soft stem Bulrush- 6 ft
Blue flag- 3 ft.
Sweet Flag- 5 ft.
Broad-leaf pond weeds-
Coontail

Floating plants
  Duck weed
  Spatterdock
  swamp smartweed
  Water Shield

  White water lily
  Yellow lotus

Fish species (that grow to over 12inches in adult size.)
  (Michigan Department of Natural resources state records)

American Eel 7.44lbs, 43inches, caught in 1990
Atlantic Salmon 32.62 lbs, 41 in, caught in 1981
Bigmouth Buffalo fish 27lbs. 35.25 in, caught 2017
Black Buffalo 44.54lbs, 38.5in, caught 2015
Black bullhead 3.44 lbs, 17 in, caught 1999
Black Crappie 4.12lbs, caught in 1983
Bluegill 2.75lbs, 13.75in caught in 1983
Bowfin 14lbs, 35in caught in 1981
Brook trout 9.5lbs, 28.1in, 1996
Brown Bullhead 3.77lbs, 17.5 in caught in 2014
Brown trout 41.45lbs, 43.75in, caught in 2009
Burbot 18.25lbs, 40in, caught in 1980
Channel Catfish 40lbs, 41.5 in, caught in 1964
Chinook salmon 46.06lbs, 43.5in caught in 1978
Cisco lake herring 6.36lbs, 21.8in caught in 2017
Coho salmon 30.56lbs, 40in, caught in 1976
Common carp 61.5lbs, 47.5in, 1974
Flathead catfish 52lbs, 46.02in, caught in 2014
Freshwater drum 28.61lbs, 34.02 in, caught in 2015
Gizzard Shad 4.12lbs, 21in, caught in 1996
Green sunfish 1.53lbs, 10in, caught in 1990
Hybrid Sunfish 1.44lbs, 11.75in caught in 1991
Kokanee salmon 1.94lbs, 18in, caught in 1978
Lake sturgeon 193lbs, 87in, caught in 1974
Lake Trout 61.5lbs, 49in, caught in 1997

Lake whitefish 14.28lbs, 31.75in, caught in 1993
Largemouth bass 11.94lbs, 27in, caught in 1934
Longnose gar 18lbs, 53in, caught in 1995
Longnose sucker 6.88lbs, 22.5in, caught in 1986
Mooneye 1.69lbs, 14.38in, caught in 1995
Muskellunge 58lbs, 59in, caught in 2012
Northern Muskellunge 49.75lbs, 51in, caught in 2000
Northern Hog sucker 2.54lbs, 19in, caught in 1994
Northern Pike 39lbs, 51.5in, caught in 1961
Pink salmon 8.56lbs, 28in, caught in 1987
Pumpkinseed 2.15lbs, 12.6in caught in 2009
Quillback 8.52lbs, 24in, caught in 2015
Rainbow trout 26.5lbs, 39.5in, caught in 1975
Red ear sunfish 2.36lbs, 12.6in, caught in 2010
Redhorse 12.89lbs, 29.25in, caught in 1991
Rock bass 3.62lbs, 20in, caught in 1965
Round whitefish menomine 4.06lbs, 21.5in, caught in 1992
Sauger 6.56lbs, 25.5in, caught in 1976
Smallmouth bass 9.98lbs, 23.1in, caught in 2016
Smelts 12in, caught in 1996
Splake 17.5lbs, 34.5in, caught in 2004
Tiger musky 51.19lbs, 54in, caught in 1919
Walleye 17.19lbs, 35in, caught in 1951
Warmouth 1.38lbs, 11in, caught in 2001
White bass 6.44lbs, 21.9in caught in 1989
White bass hybrid 10.75lbs, 27.5in, 1996
White crappie 3.39lbs, 19.5in, caught in 2000
White perch 2lbs, 13.57in, caught in 2015
White Sucker 7.19lbs, 28in, caught in 1982
Yellow bullhead 3.6lbs, 16.8in, caught in 2003
Yellow Perch 3.75lbs, 21in, caught in 1947

Non-native species
Asian Silver carp 110lbs, 55inches
Sea Lamprey 5.1lbs, 47inches.
Northern Snakeheads 17.12lbs, 4ft,11in.

Freshwater Jellyfish (Crapedacusta Sowerbyi) 5-25mm

Burbot

Lake Sturgeon

year old lake sturgeon

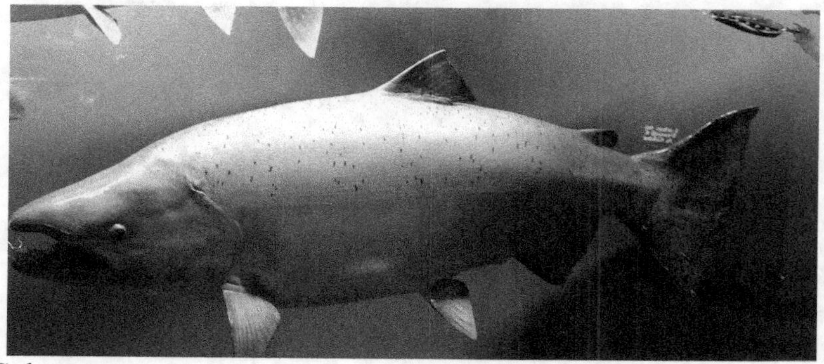

Salmon

Chapter Four

Sharks in the Great lakes.

It is well known today that Bull sharks can survive and thrive in freshwater given their ability to use their osmoregulatory process to adapt themselves to any water's salinity. The Bull shark's kidneys can gradually adjust their body to match the salt content of the waters around them.
Bull Sharks have been found thousands of miles from the oceans in freshwater rivers. Often having their pups in the brackish shallow waters. The pups may live there for a few years before migrating back out to the ocean waters.
But could a Bull shark live for any extended length of time in any of the great lakes such as Lake Michigan or Lake Superior? The Great lakes are very cold bodies of water, Even in August the water temperatures are still quite cold. Lake Erie because of it's shallow depths is the warmest of The Great lakes.
The Average surface temperatures is 25 degrees Celsius in July, August and Oct. Lake Superior averages 16 degrees Celsius in July, August and October. Lake Michigan about 21 degrees Celsius.
Bull sharks are a tropical shark species. Living in water that ranges from 21- 30 degrees Celsius. Some sharks like the Greenland sleeper shark, the Pacific sleeper shark and black

dogfish shark can live in waters as cold as 5 degrees Celsius.
 Blue Sharks, Salmon sharks,Porbeagle, Basking sharks,
Bluntnose Sixgill sharks and Spiny Dogfish can all survive arctic
waters.
 But the only shark species that have the ability to live in
freshwater are The Ganges shark, Bull shark(Carcharhihus
Leucas) and Glyphis sharks.
Some of these sharks are known for river dwelling including the
Speartooth shark(Glyphis glyphis), Borneo river shark(Glyphis
fowlerae) Ganges(Glyphis gangeticus) All of these sharks live in
and around the waters of Australia and Asia.
 So Could a Bull shark live in the Great lakes? First the shark
would have to find a river system to navigate from the ocean to in
land rivers to the great lakes. This might have been possible
before damns and seaways were built on the St.louis river,
Mississippi river and St. Lawrence river.
 The two most famous cases of Bull shark reports in the great
lakes are from Illinois. In 1937 in Alton,Illinois two fisher
named Herbert Cope and Dudge Collins caught a bullshark
measuring 5ft and weighing 84lbs. that had been raiding their
wood and wire mesh fish traps. A black and white photo exists
that show the fisherman holding their catch.

In 1955 there was a report of a bull shark attack in Lake Michigan just a short distance from Chicago. The Victim George Lawson was reportedly bite by a bull shark on his right leg. The bite was non-fatal. Witnesses claimed to have seen a large dorsal fin break the water during the attack.

This report has been viewed as valid by many sources including the World shark attack files, The TV. show River monsters and a touring museum exhibit on Megalodon shark.

In my research I decided to interview Lise Watson from the Shedd Aquarium in Chicago. Lise is the wild reef collection manager and works with sharks.

Can you tell me more about Bullsharks?

While it is well known that this species can inhabit freshwater for extended periods of time, the biggest issue here in the Midwest is the colder temperatures. Bull sharks are a tropical to subtropical species so they can tolerate cooler water but not frigid temperatures. So it is possible for this species to swim this far north and even further north but, as the temperatures drop, since sharks are cold-blooded species (there are some slight variations with species who can control their internal temperature to some degree but this doesn't apply to bull sharks) they would need to travel south to stay in a temperature range they could tolerate. We already know that Bull sharks are known to inhabit freshwater lakes and rivers around the world and I have read similar reports to the ones you've described but I can't speak as an expert on those stories since I don't have personal experience dealing with these sharks anywhere but in saltwater.

1, **In regards to the 1955 Chicago attack, was it possible that a bull shark did swim up the Mississippi river and attack the boy in lake Michigan?** It is possible, depending upon the time of the year and temperature of the water. As I mentioned above the biggest issue here is the colder water in Lake Michigan.

2. How long could a bull shark live in a fresh water ecosystem like the great lakes?

If it weren't for the temperature, it could be indefinitely.

3, If a pregnant female had pups in fresh water, would they be able to survive? Yes

4. Are there other shark species that can survive in fresh water?

Bull sharks are the only shark species that can inhabit freshwater for any length of time. Some other species of sharks enter brackish water on occasion.

5, Is it possible that bull sharks have visited the great lakes undetected in the late 1700 to 1900's?

It is possible but as I mentioned earlier they couldn't live in the cold water so they could only enter when the temperatures are warm enough and as you know, that's not too often. It's just not the most likely scenario because it doesn't really benefit them to travel this far north. While there are random reports here and there, it's not likely that any number of sharks would range this far north in freshwater. These reports obviously don't happen often and I'm not sure of how they have been substantiated so if and when occur they are considered an anomaly.

6. Have you ever heard of anyone finding a bull shark as far north as Chicago?

There are reports of bull sharks as far north as Alton, IL which is 283 miles south (4.5 hour drive) from Chicago.

There have been other reports of sharks being found washed up on the beaches of the great lakes. Most of these have been proven as pranks because the people who committed the pranks ultimately admitted to it.

Bull sharks may still swim in the Mississippi river or other rivers that drain out into the ocean but it is doubtful that they will ever be able to make it on their own into the great lakes again because of man-made barrier's.

It can also be noted that the Great lakes because of their temperatures and freshwater can not support Dolphins, Porpoises or Whales.

Chapter Five

Odd Non-native species of the Great Lakes

In the 1930's it was reported that small Jellyfish had been found living in in the great lakes. These penny-sized, clear Jellyfish are harmless. Called Craspedacusta sowerbyi, These freshwater jellyfish have been found in Lake Erie, The Huron river, Lake Huron and Lake St.Clair.

It likes shallow slow moving water to stagnant waters such as reservoirs and quarries. It was mostly likely introduces into the Great lakes by means of ornamental aquatic plants, aquatic waterfowl and stocked fish. It's native home ecosystem in the Yangtze river valley in China.

This jellyfish is harmless to people, it's micro nematocysts can not penetrate human skin. It feeds on fish eggs and insect larve.

Asian carp have been making their way up rivers towards the great lakes for years. There are 4 different species, The Bighead carp, Silver carp, Black carp and grass carp. These carp were introduced into the Southern United states in the 1970's to help support the local aquaculture.

Unfortunately The Bighead carp and silver carp have voracious appetites and ended up in the Mississippi river. These carp have decimated the local native fish populations and are known for jumping out of the water when spooked.

The Grass carp can lay between 500,000 and 3 million eggs at once and can spawn twice a year. These fish are known to have teeth and can eat between 20% to 100% of their body weight a day in plant matter, which is great for cleaning up heavy vegetation in the great lakes but very bad for native fish species that also need that vegetation to live. The Grass carp can grow to up to 55lbs as Adults.

The Bighead carp also eat vegetation and can reach lengths of 4 ft and weigh 100 or more lbs. These species were imported to help remove excess plankton from sewage treatment plants and aquaculture facilities. It is illegal to have or keep Live bighead carp in Illinois.

Silver carp are considered a threatened species in their home territory of China and Siberia. In the United states it is considered a pest. It can reach lengths of 55 inches and 110lbs. It is a filter feeder and consumes zooplanton's that native species need to survive. The Silver carp can also digest the toxic blue-green algae with out problem. Because of the consumption of that algae these carp should not be eaten by Humans.

Black carp reaches lengths of 5.9 ft and 77lbs. It's diet consist of snails and mussels. The Black carp is considered an "injurious species" under the Lacey act.

Northern Snakeheads have been horror movie stars for years since being found in American waters. This species can live outside of water for several days and the younger fish can use it's fins to "walk" on land for short distances by wriggling. The biggest Northern snakehead ever caught was 18.42 lbs. They preferr stagnant water with lots of mud and aquatic vegetation. It eats crustaceans, invertebrates and amphibians.

The Sea Lamprey is the vampire of the great lakes, It looks like an Eel with a hollywood monster mouth. It suctions onto it's host by means of a circular mouth filled with teeth. They can reach lengths of 47in and 5.1lbs.

 The sea lamprey has has become one of the apex predators of lake superior, It has destroyed the Lake trout, lake whitefish, chub and lake herring populations. Each individual sea lamprey has the ability to kill 40lbs of fish in a 12 to 18 month feeding period.

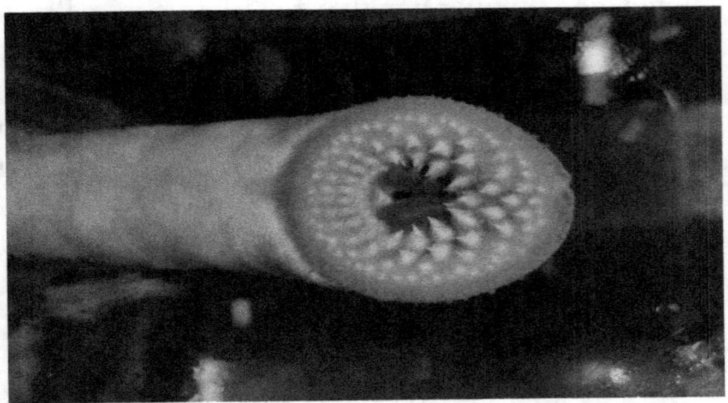

Alligators and Crocodiles

Alligator and Crocodiles have lone been a part of urban legends. People claim to see them in sewers and ponds. People once kept them as pets until they realize that they do outgrow their tanks and Bathtubs are not a good alternative.
I spoke with the owners of Critchlow Alligator sanctuary in Athens, Michigan about how often they get reports of Alligator sightings in Michigan.

1. Have there ever been any reports of alligators or similar species being let loose in ponds, lakes, rivers or the great lakes in the past or recent history

Black water township (jackson) had an alligator that was seen running around/let loose in the town. There are many reports of Alligators that are loose/seen around the state, but many times it is another animal that is mistaken as an alligator sighting. Also, in the town of Burr Oak there was an alligator found in a farmer's field about 3 summers ago. We hear about many alligators turning up, but most of the time it is because the owners don't want the alligator any longer and just let it go.

2. Has there ever been any urban legends of alligators or similar species seen or released in the Michigan or great lakes?

.Not to our knowledge have there been any alligator myths in ponds

3. Could an alligator or similar species survive our winters?

No, Alligators could not live outside in our Michigan winter. Alligators can take cold temperatures down to the 30s for short periods of time, but anything colder would kill an Alligator or any other crocodilian species.

4. Have you ever heard of any reports of giant snapping turtles?

In Ohio there is a festival dedicated about a giant snapping turtle, but as far as Michigan, I don't think so.

Monsters of Myth

Chapter Six

Native American legends about the Great lake monsters

Long before European settlers and traders came to the northern Great lakes states or tried sailing across the Great lakes the Native Americans tribes of the great lakes had long believed that the great lakes are home to some very spectacular creatures.
Oral history passed down from generation to generation retelling the stories of ancient water dwelling monsters, spirits and gods. Each tribe had their own unique tales and traditions of honoring those.
When I started researching Native American folktales of the Great lakes, I felt that it was very to with a Storyteller who was familiar with the Native stories.

1.What is your background with Native American storytelling?

My background began with a man named GrandPa George, a White Earth Cree Aniishnaab who was a Windigo Clown and Mide Elder who was the first to tell me of the 'StarMaiden' stories. He was taught by my GrandMother's people off the coast of Celebes in Indonesia after WWII. Long Story.

(http://surcadiana.blogspot.com) GrandPa was a Jiisakiiwin or Shakey Tent Medicine man. His medicine was to help veterans and alcoholics recover by sweat lodges, thirsty dances (sun dances) and a method of talking to ancestors called 'juggling' or 'shaking'.

After receiving a pipe from him, I became apprenticed to Grand Mother Mary Loomis who was a famous Jungian Psychoanalyst (https://movingboundaries.com/core/mary-loomis) who was also an Indigenous GrandMother. She was the first to tell me that my fascination and connection to StarMaiden stories from around the world. It was she who first gave me an introduction into the Native American World.

Telling and trading stories is a large part of their spiritual cultures and my people and most North and Central American tribes have an archetypally shared past and culture (Pipe, Ancestor veneration, StarMaiden/Pleiades story, Divination/prophecies). While I have had contacts with dozens of bands and tribes, it is those that have this mythology that attracts me.

2.what tribes have you learned stories from?

I started out with the local Aniishnaabeg in Michigan. GrandPa George was from Minnesota/Alberta by birth but his mother belonged to the Sault Ste Marie Ojibwa (Chippewa).
They are intermixed with Odawa (Ottawa) and Potawatomi. Many are also Cree as you go west and various forms of Algonquian as you go East. I also hold a pipe from the Anyuwiya Tsalagi Deer Clan (Eastern Cherokee) and was taught by GrandMothers who kept stories from the second Forced March and Trail of Tears by escaping to Texas (Mexico). They are a StarMaiden People and, over the years, have become mixed with Maya peoples who came up from Southern Mexico.
I hold a pipe from GrandFather American Horse of the Oglala Oyate Tiospaye that his family (along with the Afraid of Bear family) have held on (and off) Pine Ridge since it became legal to practice their religion in 1978 (rumour is that they never stopped).

GrandFather honored me for helping men in prison and at the VA in Hot Springs be allowed to sweat again.

I have pipes from the Esalen/Ohlone people in Big Sur and from the Nootka in Washington/Vancouver (sometimes called Daughters of Copper Woman). Similarly, I hold specific 'medicine wheels' from certain Quiche Maya Elders for helping bring back one of their calendars that had been destroyed.

3. What stories do you know that pertain to the native American legends of lake monsters, water spirits and gods.

I have many. StarMaiden Stories are a rough archetypal grouping of stories that have been handed down by oral tradition. They all see humans as descended from the Seventh Sister or Venus. Hold similar universal stories and cultural beliefs worldwide. My own from Celebes, for instance, is almost identical to the one told by the Lakota. Same with the Yoruba of West Africa (where my priesthood derives from) and the Greek Seven Sisters, Japanese Subaru, Celtic, Navajo, Inuit and others. These all contain the belief that the Earth was originally a 'Water Planet', that this planet or land mountain etc. was special because it contained water. Because of this, many mythologies have elements that say that we, humans, came from the water or that some of us have returned to the water. Many also contain the ideas that the oceans, rivers, lakes, etc. are filled with mythical other creatures, monsters, etc.

The Aniishnaabe are no different. Their StarMaiden came and went into a lake or pond and returned to the stars leaving all that she knew and all we needed to return in Seven Prophecies encoded on the indigenous Water Lily.

I will concentrate here on the Aniishnaabe stories and finish below with NibaNabas Manitou The first is the stories of the Water Cougars or Panthers. This is a persistent myth throughout North America. The Ojibwe say 'Mishibijiw' (Mishipeshu) and believe that they are large spiny backed creatures that prey on canoes. For some, they do not look like panthers to the Aniishnaabe, rather are called that because only big cats are

known to prey on humans. Others swear that they are big cats.
They all agree that they have large fangs or horns.
The next is the same name MissyBissy, Misabaajoo, etc. but are
huge lake monsters that are found in big lakes and are more often
described in the way we would describe Loch Ness Monster.
These are as plentiful as there are large lakes and Champ,Chessie,
Ogopogo and dozens more all point to earlier native stories.
These often are as big as whales but are depicted as having large
ornate horns. Not like a 'Plesiosaur' Nessie or Western monster.
The last (before I talk about NibaNabas) are the 'little people' of
the water.
They are called 'Paains' or apa'iinsag and different from
NibaNaabes which simply means 'water people' so they
are often interchangeable. Like the Rouge Noir of Detroit fame,
they are often small, elflike, naked or dressed in red or furry.
 They guard the water and are considred 'first ancestors'. Often,
they are appeased and venerated. They are related to the Niba
Nabas in a way I will relate below

**4. How many generations have these stories been passed
down**?

It is difficult to tell since there is no written record. Further
making it difficult is that most of these cultures are very
intermixed and their stories and names vary by area. Lately,
because of the internet, some of these stories are homogenizing
making it more difficult. We know for sure that the Mishibijiwag
in both cat and giant forms predate the Aniishnaabe since their
depictions match depictions of the Hopewell, Mississipian and the
9000 yr old un-named Copper culture of Lake Superior.
  As a vertebrate Paleontologist, my theory is that the natives here
and throughout Canada and Northeastern US are responding to
bones and whole animals found as the Post Ice Age soils,
bogs, lakes and even glaciers yielded up well preserved
'monsters' and bones. This, along with depictions, glyphs at what
have become sacred sites to them but left by previous cultures can
help explain the persistence of these stories.

When you look at the pervasive 'panther' or 'monster' stories and look at the petroglyphs you find that they are similar to two giant ancient animals. The Sturgeon and the Saber Tooth Tiger.
Both from this area and both big enough to fit the stories.
You can also make that same case for the super giant monsters. Here we have the numerous whale bones from the Great Lakes area and we also find that most 'stories' that have these contemporaneously existing with people come from out East or North (more on that in a moment). The other suspect is the great number of bog and lake monsters that were uncovered
by drought or water rerouting. Even today we get to see whole and skeletal Mammoths and Mastodons being found every day and usually in bogs or draining lakes or karns.

The last factor is that Western sailors, traders and even ancient explorers have been mixing and mating their selves and their stories. So, for instance, the Paain becomes a Lutin Rouge Noir. The NibaNabas become Sirens and suddenly Hudson Bay natives to Superior Natives are telling the tales of 'The Three Sisters'. There is even a theory that the ancient words for god
were changed because the Sun/Moon worshipping Algonquain at some point became worshippers of an invisible spirit personified as Giisis (Jesus). Not sure about that but there is a very definite Western influence in Native thought even as early as the seventeen hundreds when the French arrived.

Another fascinating mystery is who were the people of Lake Superior, who took out 9000 tons of copper when the Aniishnaabe did not use copper. It is their symbols and glyphs that first reference monsters in Lake Superior since the mines were mostly on islands far from the mainland. When you find that Native Copper from Michigan is being found in graves in Wales and Ireland, the mystery goes deeper.

All of this to say that there isn't any one definitive source, chronology or orthodoxy when it comes to native mythology. What we do know involves the stories of the NibiNaabeg or mermaids. This story is at least 500 years old as it is found in every Algonquian speaking nation as far West as Seattle, as far

south as the Navajo in AZ and as far south as Georgia. The
Aniishnaabe migration began 500 years ago from the St.
Lawrence Seaway and because their migration prophecy was
about the Miigis (Cowrie Shell) the clans or 'doodems' (totems)
that preserved their teachings and healings have always been the
Giishkizhigwan or water nation (clans all named after sea life)
and specifically the clan called the Nibinaabeg or 'water people'.

5. Do you believe or think that these stories had actual real life creatures or animals?

Yes, as I described above when talking about age, I do believe
that there are reasonable guesses as to some of the sources.
Mermaids and Little People are more problematic. There is
no ancient animal or fossil, no plausible proofs and, yet, their
existence is world wide and very uniform in who they are, what
they look like and even their personalities and purpose.
Merpeople are not so easy. While they are easily the most
pervasive of all the stories, there is no actual scientific
possibilities or conjectures. On the other hand, they are part of
every culture that has a StarMaiden Mythology or a Sirius based
mythology (like the Dogon in West Africa).

6. In a recent discussion with another paleontologist, He mentioned that some tribes who are nomadic brought whales bones in the great lakes region. Do you think this may have contributed to the creation of stories of lake monsters?

Not really. If you think about that for a second, you see that you
would need the whole whale to tell that tale. We know bones were
brought but it is much simpler to believe that whale bones
already existed here and everywhere in what was once the great
central sea called the Michigan Illinois Basin. Along with any
number of other animals that fit the bill. If you add whole
intact animals being pulled from bogs and glaciers, it is more
likely that these animals actually appeared and, because of their
location, suppositions were made. Imagine finding a six foot rib

bone or a mammoth skull with ten foot tusks.

I know some tribes that refer to Sturgeon as Miisabajoo and since Sturgeon will continue to grow as long as they have space and food, they can grow as large as 7000 lbs. And they have two large protruding spines from their mouths.

7. What is your understanding or interpretation of the Native American Great Lakes Water God Manitou Niba Nibis?

I think the first thing we have to do is define what we are talking about. Manitou does NOT mean God. Until Westerners came, the natives here used the term to indicate that a thing was very sacred. A pipe is manitou but so is water. Here, it means a sacred and mysterious being. One of many. Thunderers. Cannibalistic Windigo. Bagwajiwininiwag, 'WildMen' or Sasaquatch, Wemicus trickster spirits and many more are all considered 'manitou' or sacred. But they are not 'gods'. They are elements or powerful facets of Gichi Manitou which is All things Sacred. Everything but in Balance and Mysterious and As It Should Be. Everything And not an anthropomorphic old man or 'god'.

'Nibi' means 'Water'. Naabe (like AniishNaabe) means people. Because Ojibwe is largely an unwritten language you have many variations. Nibinabe, Nibanaba, Nibanabe, Ne-bo-na-bee, Niba Nabais, Nebaunaube, Negaunabe. The plural form is Nibiinaabeg (also spelled Neebananbaig or Ne-ban-a-baig.) Nibiinabekwe is a feminine form of the same word.

They all refer to a half person half fish. It is now applied to water elfs or Apa'iinsag but that is not accurate except that they both have a relation to water. The Nibanabag are the 'water people' in much the same way that the Lakota say 'stone people', 'tree nation' etc. They are a distinct race and are not considered as gods until after the European synchronization. They are a type of human. We often see that when French Fur traders tell these stories they are less apt to be changed to make moral judgments as is often the case when Catholic missionaries are the story scribes.

The story that most interests me is a NanaBozoo story.
Longfellow wrote many of these stories down but changed the
name of Nana Bozoo to Hiawatha. He told it as almost a novel
tale about
one person's one tale but the actual stories are many and are
closer to 'Brer Rabbit' tales in that he is often used to explain
history or morals like a fable. Very often his stories belong to no
particular time and may be told as if he were a living 'friend', an
'ancient historical character' or a 'mythical being'. He is
sometimes human, sometimes a shapeshifter. Often a trickster.
Whatever the story requires.
He is sometimes called MishaWabazhoo and that means 'Great
Rabbit' and his stories are often like the 'Brer Rabbit' stories of
the North Carolina Gullah slaves who also told wolf, coyote and
fox tales. Their stories were recorded in the seventeen hundreds
already and already mixed freely with Angolan and Yoruba tales.
    This is how we know that these tales predate western
influence because they are persistent as far south as Georgia and
as far north as Hudson Bay.
NanaBzoo was the first Aniishnabeg. The first human. This is
how that came to be. You see, his mother was called WeNoNah
which means 'first born daughter' we do not say her real name for
she has walked over. Passed. Gone. She was of the NibiNaabeg,
the 'water people'.
 Her own mother had fallen from a Star long ago and chose to
swim with the fish as this world had more water than anything.
We just call her GrandMother or Nokomis.
WeNoNah was beautiful and longed to walk upon the land and
swim in the streams and lakes far from her great water. It was on
one of these 'walks' that she was spied by Mudjekeewis,
which means 'first born son', He, the Great Bear from the West.
He spied her getting out of the waters and slipping out of her fish
skin to reveal her legs and walk about. He fell in love with her
and decided to hide her skin so she would not leave. When they
met, she was looking for her fish skin and he lied and said that he
would help her find them.

They never did find them but they, instead, fell in love and she
bore him a son. It was not long, however, before she fell ill
because she did not belong on the earth and when Mudjekeewis
realized this, he brought her skin to her but it had dried up and
when she realized that he had lied to her, her heart broke and she
died.

The great mourning bear took the little hairless bear to the water's
edge and he wept as he placed his wife on a bed of lilies. As she
sank into the depth of the water, another woman arose
from the water and into the air from a fish, to a bird, to a butterfly
and then into an old lady.

She said not a word but silently took the baby from the Great
Bear and realized that she could not take him into the water
because he did not know how to change yet. So she raised him
amongst the little people who lived by the water and, in time, he
took many wives and had many children. Each in the guise of a
different animal.

 Each of these animals are the clans of the people today.

Each generation, Nokomis (which means 'My Grandmother')
took one child of the water people clan and raised him as Nana
Bzhoo 'the one who changes'. She believed that he would be the
one to decipher the meaning of the Star Lily that would take them
back to the stars when the Seventh Prophecy came true.

 When Nokomis died it was upon the people to remember her
ways but, as often happens, the Old Ones forgot or turned their
backs on Her Ways. The Seventh Prophecy foretold of that time.
But it also foretold of the coming of children who would not need
to be taught. They would remember. They would either bring the
Way of the Stars to the Earth or, if the Sacred Waters were
despoiled, they would find their Way Home to the Stars.

This is the story of The StarMaiden. The Lakota story is similar
but with Seven Sisters.

 So is the tale of the StarMaiden from my people, the Tana Toraja.
Seal Skin Soul Skin of the Inuit People. Gidi Gidi of the Odu Ifa
peoples and so many more. As a priest of the African tradition,
my life is ruled by a divination tale. Just like GrandMother Mary

and GrandPa George foretold a dozen years before, it is a story of a StarMaiden who is a mermaid who falls to earth and loses her head. She is doomed to live under the ground where the underground hot-streams meet the oceans. She lives in a cave awaiting the day when the moon will cross the tiny opening far above her and she can find her way out and back to the stars. These are those times…

7. I was wondering if you had any information about Manitou Niba Nibis, the native American God of the great lakes. I found the name mentioned in an old report about a lake creature dwelling in Lake Superior.

Let me ask a friend. It means 'water water' indicating very large water. It also means 'I sleep water' or 'I perish water'. This is different from the water panther and water thunder beings. It is more like a great black water death that snatches you off the shore. Some call it Pressie but that is more like a plesiosaur. My Aniishnabe friend says it is like rip tide or a large black presence under water. but let me ask around.The report stated it was the name of a child size merman that was seen swimming off shore. The native American women with the group called it Manitou Niba Nibis In the area around the islands of North West Lake superior Let me check. I'm very into mermaid mythology and I would be very curious. Manitou means 'spirit' or god. My friend tells me that they are call nibinaabe or 'water people'. He said that there are clans who say they are descended from them and that they are just like western or African merfolk. Half human and half fish. I will see if I can find out more
My friend, who is an aniishnab in Canada, tells me that mermaid and sea monster tales are centered on the east coast. Aniishnabe are Algonquian speakers and much of their lore comes from Eastern Canada.
Here, the stories sound suspiciously like Norse stories. My friend, an archaeologist, thinks that both French and Viking contact predate Columbus and you have many Algonquian words that sound like archaic French and Norse. Giisis (Jesus) and

Bazhoo(Bon Jour) chief among them.
Here, is a link he sent:
http://www.sacred-texts.com/nam/ne/al/al57.htm

There are so many different Monsters, spirits and gods from the many different tribes that it can become confusing as to which name belongs to which one. I spent many weeks comparing notes and researching each one.

Misshepezhieu is Ojibwe, Also called Mishipizheu, Mishipizheu, Mishupishu, Mishepishu, Michipeshu or Mishibijiw. These are all the Great water Lynx or Lake Superior's great water dragon.
They are the opposing force in the thunderbird story. They exist in the deepest part of the lakes and rivers. They are an amalgamation of many animals. Like the cougar, deer and eagle.
Some legend say that the Misshepezhieu is a protective creature, while others legends claim that it brought death to those who dared to steal it's copper.

Gichi-anami'e-bizhiw also Ojibwe for The Fabulous water panther.

Mishebeshu the Ojibwe water monster also referred to as the Great Lynx. It lives in an underwater den near the mouth of the Serpent river that flows into Lake Huron.

Michi Peshu is the Anishinabe spelling for the work Great underwater Lynx.

Mishipashoo also Anishinabe for Great underwater Lynx.

Nibiinaabe are Anishinabe water spirits. They are also called Nibinabe, Nibanaba, Nibanabe, Ne-bo-na-bee, Niba Nabais, Nebaunaube, Negaunabe. The plural form is Nibiinaabeg (also spelled Neebananbaig or Ne-ban-a-baig.) Nibiinabekwe is a feminine form of the same word. These names are used by

Ojibwe, Algonquin, Potawatomi and Menominee tribes.

Gaasyendietha is a water dragon that lives in Lake Ontario according to Seneca tribe legends. This Dragon flew on a trail of fire and could spew fire.
It was also known as the Meteor dragon and legend says it fell as a meteoroid and impacted with the earth. The explanation of the dragon was given to French explorer Jacques Cartier by Seneca natives when Cartier inquired as about a creature he and his crew sighted. They described the creature as a giant blue finned snake.

Maymaygwashi is an Ojibwe merman. Said to hide among underwater rocks. It has 6 fingers on each hand and a brown skin tone. It is also called **Nebauaubaewuk**.

Misiginebig is the underwater horned serpent of the Algonquian tribes. It is also called Mishiginebig, Mishi-Ginebig, Meshkenabec, Msi-Knebik, Kichikinebik, Kichiginebig, Mishi-Kinebig, Mishikinebik, Misikinebik, Meshkenabec, Mshignebig, Kchiknebig, Mshiknebik, Kchiknebik, Kichiknebik, Kchiknebig, Kchiginebig, Mshiginebig, Misi-Ginebig, Misiganebic, Miciginabik, Miciginabig, Micikinebik, Mecikenäpikwa, Maeci-Kenupik, Maec-Kenupik, Meqsekenaepik, Misikinubick, Misikinubik, Meshe-Kinebik, Meshekenabek, Misi-Kinebik, Mi'shikine'bik, Mi'siki'nipik, Misikinebik, Msi-Kinepikwa, Msí kinépikwa, Misi-Kinopik, Ktchi-Kinepikwa, Me'cigenepigwa, Misiganebic, Mi:'s-kenu:pik, Msi-kinepeikwa, Kinepikwa, Misikinipik, Psikinepikwa, Psikinépikwa, Genay-big, Mah-she-ken-a-peck by the Ojibwe, Algonquian, Ottawa, Menominee, Shawnee, Cree tribes.

Manitou Niba Nibis the God of lakes and waters. Reported by fur traders as looking mermaid like.

Onaire is a dragon-like horned water serpent of Iroquois. It is also called Onyare, Onyarhe, On-yar-he, O-ni-a-re, Oniares, Ohnyare, Ohnyare:kowa; Oniont, Oneyont, Angont; Donongaes, Doonogaes, Doonongaes; Jodi'gwadon.
 It is the mortal enemy of the thunder god Hinon. The name Onyare means snake in Mohawk and Onyarekowa mean Great snake. Legend says it would tip canoes and devour the people in it. Passengers could be save if they made an offering before going onto the lakes.

Water Panther names from the Ojibwe, Algonququin, Ottawa, Menominee, Shawnee and Cree tribes. Mishibizhiw, Mishibizhii, Mishipeshu, Mishipizheu, Mishibijiw, Mishipizhiw, Mshibzhii, Mshibzhiw, Mishipizhu, Misipisiw, Mishipiishiiw, Messibizi, Missipissy, Mitchipissy, Michipichi, Mishibizhi, Michipizhiw, Mishupishu, Mishepishu, Michipeshu, Misibizhiw, Michipichik, Msipissi, Msi-Pissi, Msipessi, Missibizi, Michi-Pichoux, Gichi-anami'e-bizhiw, Gitche-anahmi-bezheu, Nampeshiu, Nambiza, Nampèshiu, Nampe'shiu, Nambi-Za, Nampeshi'kw, Nambzhew, Naamipeshiwa, Namipeshiwa, Nah-me-pa-she, Peshipeshiwa, Manetuwi-Rusi-Pissi, Manetúwi Msí-Pissí, Maeci-Pesew, Matc-Piseo, Wiä'bskinit Mätc Pis'eu

(Mishibeshu petroglph drawing at Agawa rock, Lake Superior Provincial park, Ontario, Canada)

The Legend of the Great Water Lynx

The great enemy of the Thunderbird. The battles were so fierce that great storms would be created on the Great lakes when they fought. The Mishibeshu would churn up the waters with it's long copper tail and the Thunderbird would shoot down lighting bolts to stop it.

These storms would overturn canoes and drown the passengers. The reason for Mishibeshu's anger was often attributed to people stealing his copper and not making offerings. Many copper laiden vessels have sunk and lay at the bottom of the great lakes. The Algonquian and Ojibwe tribes claim thie shape-shifting spirit lives at the very bottoms of the deepest parts of each great lake. Mishibeshu had horns and a tail made from copper, The body of a panther and spikes proturding from it's neck and back. It also lives near Michipicoten Island in Lake Superior.

A Jesuit missionary named <u>Claude Dablon</u> told a story about four Ojibwa Indians who embarked on a journey to the home of *Mishibeshu* to take some copper back to their home, and use it to heat water. The very second they pushed off and backed into the water with their canoe, the eerie voice of the Mishibeshu surrounded them. Then Mishibeshu came growling after them, vigorously accusing them of stealing the playthings of his children. All four of the Indians died on the way back to their village; the last one surviving just long enough to tell the tale of what had happened in his final moments before he died.

Monsters of Legend

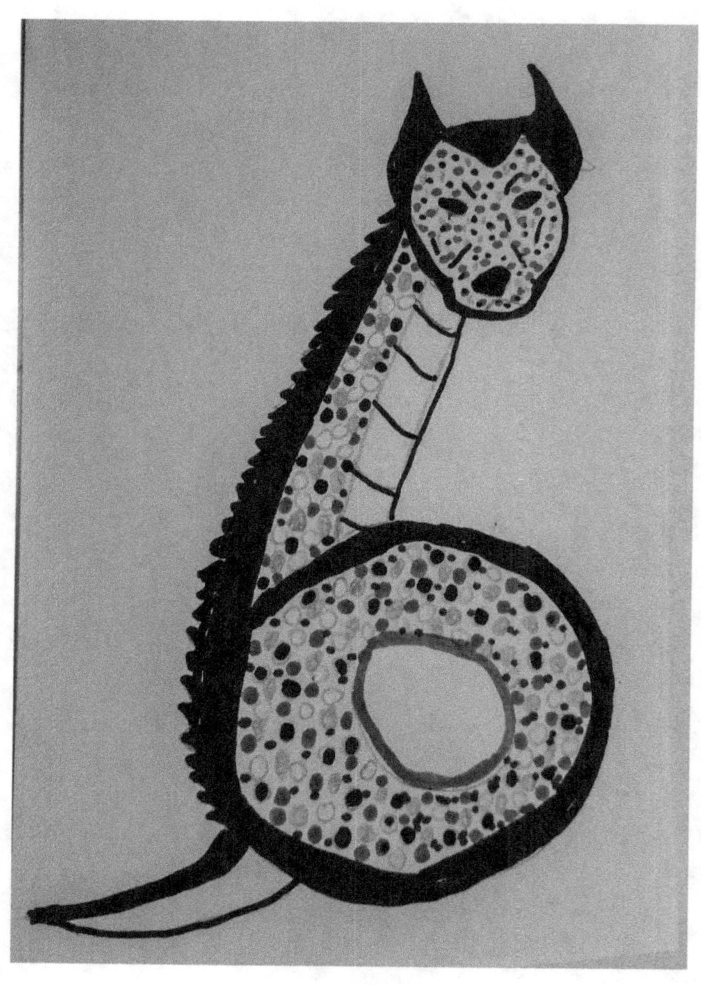

Chapter Seven

Lake monsters sightings of the Great lakes.

Lake Huron sightings.

Spring 1989, Easter Sunday
St.Ignace, Michigan
A husband and wife spotted a large wake heading northeast
towards Rabbit's back point. After looking through powerful
binoculars. They observed what looked like a submarines
periscope 2 feet above the waters surface.

August 1975
 reports of a 40ft snakelike creature swimming north from
Cheboygan were reported.

June 1976
Cheboygan, Michigan. 15 miles south of the Straits of Mackinaw
Reports of a sea monster were made to the local sheriffs. Snake
like creatures measuring 40ft long were seen swimming about
600ft. Off shore. The following day a deputy was sent out to

investigate and saw a creature 20 to 30 ft long swimming just below the surface. Another deputy was sent out into the water on a canoe to investigate but could not get close enough to the creature before it disappeared.

1975
Kincardine, Ontario. Southern end of lake Huron
Witnesses reported a huge school of mysterious creatures.

1989
Goderich
two long log like creatures were spotted swimming in the lake.

October 24th, 1890
F.E. Bradley sawmill, near Detroit, Michigan
A monster snake was sighted at night by the sawmill workers. More reports claimed it had a dead glow in its eyes and measured 12ft long, Plus had an ox shaped head. It can be noted that a local museum had just burned down and loss it large Anaconda.

1960's
Summer
a huge creature was seen swimming up the St.Mary's river by an entire family. Undulating humps were seen just above the water.

1897 Summer
Sarnia, Ontario 3 miles offshore
A group of men from Detroit were fishing in 145ft of water when their boat began moving at a rapid speed, as if something had their anchor line. Suddenly a "black mass, a swift moving ribbon shaped monster, dashed to the surface. One of the men fired his revolver at the creature and the water was lashed into a bloody foam. The monster was at least 88ft long with a double rows of fins and had long whiskers.

October 1938
Sarnia and South Hampton, Ontario
6 sober Fisherman claimed to run their boat ashore in order to
avoid a huge sea serpent. 30 Ft long and moving in an
undulating manner with a menacing tail that swished back and
forth. In 1937 a similar creature was reported 100 miles to the
north.

1938
Wasage beach, Nottawasaga bay.
A 8ft long seal like creature was reported.

July 23, 1948
Georgian bay near Flowerpot island
Several witnesses aboard the excursion steamer City of Detroit III reported seeing a 60ft green and purple scaled monster. It came within 500 ft of the steamer and was watched for a total of 15 minutes.

August 16, 1897
Belle Isle, Michigan
A lake captain reportedly captured a sea serpent near the foot Joseph Campeau Ave. It was described as having a mouth as big as a coal stove. Fast moving and hissing. The Captain killed the monster with a boat hook. Claiming the serpents jaws distended, turned and swam at the Captain. Its tail lashing the water. The monster measured 17ft long and 2 ft wide.

Saggie/Saggy
Saginaw bay monster
A monster that lurks in Saginaw bay off of Lake Huron.

1892
Straits of Mackinac
A group of women spotted a black, oily skinned snake like creature while bathing in the water. The serpent ignored the women and made a whirring sound.

Summer 1897
Lake St.Clair

A group of men left their horses near the shoreline while they rowed out to fish. They were startled to hear blood curdling whinnies from the spot where they left their horses. A sea serpent had been sighted coming ashore and dragging the poor horse to it's watery death.

August 6 1897
Sandwich point, Detroit river
A sea serpent measuring 87ft. Long with a bull-like head and
magnificent pair of antlers. It also had one single eye
in the center of its forehead.

Lake Ontario

July 3, 1817
Lake Ontario
Schooner crew reported seeing a sea serpent about 3 miles
offshore. It looked to be a 1 ft in diameter and 35 to 40 ft long.
Its skin almost black.

Fur trading days
Toronto,Canada
A boat returned to Toronto after encountering a great snake about
20 miles from Niagara, Ontario. The passengers reported seeing a
great snake of at least 30ft in length. The reports were made to the
local Magistrates.

 August 5, 1829
Ten Mile creek, Western Ontario.
Several children playing near the mouth of the creek claimed they
saw a monster snake, that was 20 to 30 feet long and had a head
that was 10 to 15 inches in diameter.

Kingston, Ontario is a hot bed of sea monsters sightings. Locals
call their sea serpent "Kingstie" There was a time when Boat
Captains planned together and tried to catch the monster known
as Kingstie.

The Vessels Diamond of Napanee, Adventure of Kingston,
Ivanhoe of Napanee and Norman of Belleville were all working
together to capture the creature, so that they could sell it to
P.T.Barnum

September 1881
A serpent was sighted by the passengers and crew of the steamer
Gypsy. It was estimated to be 25 to 40 ft long with small legs and
a large tail. The creature was reported to be faster than the
Steamer.

June 1888
Wolfe and Simcoe Islands
Two men sailing in the channel, sighted a sea serpent for a brief
time.

July 1892
Brakey's bay
A man and his wife sailing in a skiff were attacked by huge
serpent that had eyes like balls of fire. The husband fought the
serpent off using his fishing pole.

August 1931
Alexandria Bay
Two medical doctors sighted a creature they thought to be 30 ft.
long. It had a single eye in the middle of it's head and had two
antler-like horns.

July 1, 1833
Kingston, Ontario
Captain Kellogg claimed to have seen a huge serpent.175 ft long
and dark blue in color with brown spots. As wide as a barrel of
 flour and tapered at each end. It swam in an undulating motion.

July 25, 1821
100 miles from Niagara, Lake Ontario
John Maupin and and James Sigler, Jefferson county, New york
Canoe named the Light-foot The 8 person crew spotted a body
floating some 500 to 600 yards away. The creature seem to be
asleep and look to be 20-25ft. Long. When the canoe came about
30 yards from the creature, It lifted it's head about 10ft, out of the
water.

The party decided to fire at the serpent and loaded their guns. The canoe moved slowly towards it and watched as it sprang to life, They realized it was 37ft. Long and 2 ½ ft. diameter and covered in black scales. With a tremendous head and very snake like tongue that looked venomous.

The legend of Mike Finn and the Lake Ontario monster.

Mike Finn was well known for his tall tales and stories of conquest. Mike Finn often told these tales to the amusement of his local bar friends. Mike was a happy go lucky, fun loving Irishmen who live in the city Oswego. One night while retelling his tales, a stranger came into the bar and asked him about Monsters?

"Monsters" Mike shouted "Monsters, well now, my friend, there are no such things. But if there were I would not be afraid of them."

"How do You know there are no such things" the stranger
inquired
"Why, Why because there are no such things" Mike said, "only in
fairy tales about giants, ogres and monsters"
 The stranger then proceeded to tell Mike and his friends about a
Monster that was living near Rome swamp. That the monster had
come down from Canada following the French Canadians.
The monster was called the Carcagna.
The Carcagna was described as looking like a Dragon with
terrible red eyes and a snake like body that was covered with
slimy seaweed that never stopped dripping. It had huge Orange
wings with black and brown feathers sticking onto them. People
claimed that if you heard it's terrible cry, you would go mad and
 never be the same.
Mike Finn and his buddies listened the strangers story and
laughed abit. The Monster was of no concern to them because it
lived in a far away swamp.
But the Stranger next words were cause for alarm. The creature
was moving towards their location. It had been seen two nights
before wailing and crying as it headed towards the Port of
Ontario.
The night before it was heard by a fishing boat near Scriba.
The Stranger claimed that Carcagna would soon be swimming
into Oswego Harbor that very night.
The Stranger then claimed that no one had ever heard the creature
and stayed sane to tell about. This was a channel Mike Finn was
willing to take.
So at 7 o clock that very night, Mike Finn set out in his little
rowboat to spend the night on Lake Ontario. Just outside of
Oswego Harbor.
 Or so He had told his friends. He really only planned to row out
passed the Lighthouse, Then wait until darkness fell and make for
the shoreline. His friends knew this was his plan so they followed
him to the Harbor entrance and patrolled it all night.
The Following morning at first light They all gathered on the
docks and waited. The two men who had last patrolled the Harbor
claimed to have no seen Mike Finn that night.

The whole group was getting ready to set out on a search party of all the local coves when an object was seen bobbing on the water in the far distance.

Several boats were launched in an attempt to recover Mikes boat and many stood on the end of the pier. Watching! As Mikes boat was towed to the dock the men in the other boats were gray faced and very seriously.

As the boats came into Dock, the witnesses saw Mike Finn curled up in a ball on the bottom of his rowboat. His hair was now snow white, his eyes were fixed and his smile made a terrible grin. His teeth chattering the whole time.

As they pulled Mike from the boat and walked him ashore, some men decided it best to drydock Mike's rowboat. But they were stunned when a single slimy black and brown feather was found on the boats floor.

Could The Carcagna also have been the Gaasyendietha?

Lake Michigan

August 9, 1867
Michigan city, Lake Michigan
Boats involved: The tugboat George W. Wood and the propeller Sky Lark.
An animal measuring 40 to 50 ft long with a serpentine shape.
With a neck as thick as a Human being and it's body as wide as a barrel.

1892
Muskegon Harbor, Lake Michigan
A diver spotted a serpent coiled around a ships rudder underwater.
It looked to be 60ft. Long and dark color.

The Lake Michigan triangle

The Lake Michigan triangle is located in the middle of the lake Michigan. The triangle starts in Ludington, then goes to Benton Harbor Then across to Manitowoc, Wisconsin then back to Ludinton, Michigan
 Numerous strange disappearances of land, air and watercraft. Ufo's, Ghost ship sightings, Sea serpents have all been witnessed for a long time.
 Over 40 planes have disappeared over Lake Michigan. The Most famous being Flight 2501. The plane was headed to Minneapolis from New York city in June 1950. It plunged into Lake Michigan just off of Benton Harbors shoreline. No wreckage has ever been found.

Lake Erie

1793
Middle Bass Island north of Sandusky, Ohio
Boat: sloop Felicity
A party of explorers reported many large rattlesnakes, At the time
the island seemed infested with rattlesnakes. The Captain claimed
to have seen a monstrous snake more than 16 ½ feet in length.

July 1817
Lake Erie, 5 mile from shore
A 40ft long serpent that was dark in color was seen.
The water snake of Lake Erie was born.

July 1873
Buffalo, New York. It was part whale and had a water spout. It
had small eye and a broad mouth with two rows of teeth. It swam
at about 10 mph.
Afterwards a local farmer discovered strange tracks and drag
marks on the shore and into the water. The men hired a tugboat
and went out hunting for the monster.
They spied a movement in the water and opened fire. The water
churned and foamed and the Monster rose from the water with a
hideous scream. Its eyes blazing like coals. Then it sank from
sight.

July 30, 1880
Erie, Pennsylvania
Boat: Schooner General Scott
A sea serpent was seen 30 miles from Erie, Pennsylvania. The
crew described is as being 40ft. Long with a neck about 10 to
12 inches in diameter. The skin was dull mahogany colored,
almost black.

May 1877
Locust point, Ottawa County, Ohio
The Dusseau brothers saw a large phosphorescent mass lying on

the beach. They described it as a Lake monster, writhing in agony.

It resembled a large sturgeon and had long arms. The brothers claimed that it was 20 to 30ft long. It looked to have died and the brothers went to get a rope to drag it further up the beach. When the brothers returned, The monster was gone. The only evidence was large silver scales left.

July 1892
Toledo,Ohio
Boat: Madeline
Skipper Captain Woods reported that he and his crew spotted a huge sea serpent wrestling in the water with an unknown foe, The seen Serpent was estimated to be 50ft. Long and 4 ft in diameter. Its head was raised 4 feet above the water and had vicious sparkling eyes with a large head. Fins were seen on the monster and its skin was dark brown in color.

October 1894
Silver creek , New York
Reverend Alex Watt and his wife, accompanied by another women were paralyzed with astonishment when a creature appeared 15 ft from shore. Running down the serpents back were two rows of fins about 1 foot apart. The monster also had fins about a foot long. It skin was dark colored and it had a huge head.

May 1896
Crystal Beach, Fort Erie Ontario
Four people seen what they described as a giant fish moving through the waters. The creature seemed to be headed for the nearby beach but never came ashore.
They watched it for 45 minutes before it disappeared into the dark. It had eyes the size of Silver dollars. It's head was dog like but the tail was like a monstrous land serpent. It measured 30 ft. long.
One of the men was Captain Beecher and he pick up stones to throw at the monster but the monster reacted as if the stones were

toys and chased after the stones and caught them in his mouth.

July 1896
Port Dover, Ontario
A boy named C.D. Woolley saw a hideous monster about a half mile out. 9 feet of its body were out of the water and it carried itself in a reptilian manner. He guessed it was 30ft. Long.

20th century
Long Point,
A monster with a head like a horse. A boat skipper chased the monster, much to his crews horror. They never caught the monster as it dove under the water.

July 1983
Sandusky, Ohio
A women named Mary heard something paddling through the water on a foggy morning. Then she saw what she described as an capsized rowboat moving slowly through the water. She saw a huge back like a turtle shell about 30 to 35 ft. long and dark green in color and smelled a stench like rotting garbage.
The Creature had a huge head, almost prehistoric looking.

Summer 1985
Vermillion, Ohio
A dark brown serpent with a flat tail was spotted by some boaters. People claimed 5 humps rose above the water.
A Few days later a man saw the same creature near Lorain Coast Guard station. He said it was twice as long as his 16ft. Boat.

1990's
Bessie is named the Lake Erie monster and South Bay Bessie is born.

May or June of 1989, Gail Kasner obtained a graph from a boat owned by Ken Smith of Streetsboro. The fishfinder appeared to show a sonar reading of a cigar shape apparition about 35 feet in length at a depth of about 30 feet.

July 8, 1990, Susan Seeson, of Salem witnessed the creature two miles from Cedar Point. Her description basically matched other reports.

September 3, 1990, Bob Soracco was jet skiing off Port Clinton when he thought he spotted a porpoise, he did not know that porpoise did not live in Lake Erie as he had just moved from Florida. He told reporters that he saw humps with gray spots. "It was very long as I moved closer and it was going down."

September 4, 1990, Harold Bricker and his family were fishing north of Cedar Point Amusement Park when a serpent like creature swam by their boat about 1000 feet away They described it as 35 feet long with a snake like head. It moved as fast as their boat. Later, the Brickers reported their sighting to the ODNR rangers at East Harbor State Park.

September 11, 1990, Fire inspectors, Jim Johnson and Steve Dircks of Huron, saw the creature from a third story window facing Lake Erie. They described it as dark blue or black at about 30 to 45 feet long. He further stated that he saw three parts of the creature above water. "It laid there motionless for three to six minutes and was flat on top."

September 16, 1991, Dennis Szececinski, of Toledo saw Bessie near Toledo's water intake structure three miles offshore in Maumee Bay. He was fishing in the bay when something long and black slithered in front of him.

Summer 1993
3 separate reports of the a sea serpent were made, A family of 4, saw a creature close to the shoreline of Lowbanks, Ontario. A 30 foot snake like creature was seen swimming nears Kelleys Island by two different fishermen on separate days.

August 24, 1993
A group of Ohio business men offered up a reward of $102,700
in cash and prizes for the capture or evidence of the creature,
After an article was published in the Weekly World News
claiming a 38ft. Sailboat was crushed by a 200 ton sea monster.

August 2001
Port Dover, Ontario
Several people were attacked and visiously bitten on their legs
while swimming in the area. A Doctor who examined the victims
reported that the puncture wounds were major, measuring 6inches
between the upper and lower teeth..

Bessie of Lake Erie
Bessie is described as a 30-40 foot long serpent. Dark in color and
1-2 feet in diameter. It moves it's body in a vertical undulating
motion and moves through water very quickly. The Seneca tribe
have legends of similar creatures that they claim live in Lake Erie
and the Niagara river.
On July 22, 1931, the Register reported that sea serpent had been
captured in the waters of Sandusky Bay. A New York Times
reporter who happened to be visiting the town that Tuesday
picked up on the story. The story which followed stated that two
fishermen from Cincinnati, Clifford Wilson and Francis
Cogenstose, noticed the creature as it surfaced near their boat
earlier that day. Frightened the two men beat the beast over the
head with an oar, knocking it unconscious. They then fastened a
line to the creatures head and towed it to shore.

As their catch began to regain consciousness Wilson and
Cogenstose obtained a packing box, 6 feet long, 3 feet wide and
about 2 feet deep, and coiled the creature in, nailing on the cover
for safety. As the numerous scoffers gathered around the box
neither the beasts captures or any of the curious onlookers would
chance opening the box for fear of being attacked. Police Captain
Leo Schively, C.J. Irwin and Mel Harmon, of the Sandusky
morning paper, and E.L. Ways, managing editor of a local
afternoon paper, claimed that they saw the serpent as it was being

boxed up and joined the fishermen in describing it as a large, snake like beast, with a black, dark green and white hide resembling that of an alligator.

Word of Bessie's capture made its way to Harold Madison, the curator of the Cleveland Museum of National History, who traveled to Sandusky to examine the catch, and determined that the beast was nothing more than an Indian Python. Wilson and Cogenstose quickly skipped town and further investigation revealed that the men, one of whom had family ties in Sandusky, worked for a touring carnival. Despite all of these hoaxes Bessie lived on, being sighted in 1960, 1969, 1981, 1983, 1985 and 1989. A flurry of sightings were reported in 1990 including a sighting by two Huron firefighters.

The Storm Hag of Lake Erie.
Legend goes that a siren lived in the bottom of Lake Erie. The Storm Hag has yellow eyes, green teeth and skin. Her fingernails are poisonous. She is blamed for calling storms in with her voice and attacking sailors and ships.
After sinking the ships, she takes them to her home on the Lake's bottom.

Lake Superior

The giant sturgeon of Chippewa legend.

The Great lakes Chippewa tribe believed that a giant sturgeon lived in Lake Superior. Its mouth was big enough to fit an entire village inside it. The great sturgeon was often blamed for missing canoes and the passengers.
Not even early schooners were immune, While white settlers blames the ship losses on squalls. The Chippewa knew better.
to them all it took for a schooner to sink was the mild flick of the great sturgeon's tail.
In 1909 a 250 foot steel hauled steamer ship the Leafeld was

crossing Lake Superior on a perfect summer day. The Lake was peaceful and calm, not a cloud in the sky. Suddenly Lake Superior unleashed a furious storm.

The waves that boiled all around the Leafeld punished the steamed unmercifully. For 20 to 30 minutes the windless storm battle the Leafeld. Then just as suddenly as the storm had started, it was done. The crew later found out that an earthquake had occurred, But seeing at the Steamer had been moving through the lake at the point where it reached 1000ft deep. The old timers held beliefs that the storm was cause by something else.

Winter 1909
The 504 foot steamer James E Davidson had similar events happen to it. During a snowstorm near the Slate island, A single massive wave smashed down onto the Steamer without warning. The force was so great that it knocked the Sailors off their feet and launched both of the forward anchors from their pockets. The thunderous sounds of hundreds of feet of chain and anchor crashing into the depths of lake Superior was deafening. The hawse holes were damaged and the forward hold filled with water as the front of the ship sunk forward. It barely made it into port. Upon examination a 10 foot dent was found under the bow of the boat.

The steamer Emperor was upbound from the SOO when it experience an odd event. Using coal that had been recovered from a wreck. The the coal was wet and not burning well so the Captain ordered the grates to be cleaned. The steamer added water ballast to keep from rolling. The Steamer sat unmoving in 1000ft of water when the Steamer bumped something solid and slide off it.

In 1928 the steamer Midland Prince also hit something solid in the same area. In 1929 The Superior shoal was found and many blamed these collisions with the Ships hitting the shoals.

May 13, 1782

Lake Superior's thunder bay Pie Island

Members of the North West company spotted what they described as a "Merman". After making camp on the southern end of the island, the party set out some fishing nets . Once back onshore the party noticed an animal in the waters just off the beach. It appeared to have the upper body of a human being and below the waist looked to be finned. It was the size of an 8 yr. Old child and looked to be male. It had brownish complexion and human like arms.

When the Leader of the group tried to shoot his musket at the great, An old Squaw stopped him. She informed the man Mr. Venant St. Germain that, that was indeed the God of the lakes and waters, The God Manitou Niba Nibais. She also told the party that since they had all looked upon the creature, That now they were all doomed.

As the creature disappeared back under the waves, the old squaw was very shaken. She refuse to walk back up the beach to camp and insisted that a great storm was now headed for them.

She made her way up a very steep incline and took a higher path back to the campsite.

For the next 3 day, a furious storm battered the party as they waited on land for it to pass.

This whole event was reported to 2 judges of the court of the King's bench in Montreal, Quebec.

July 1895
Whitefish point, Michigan
The steamer ship the SS Curry crew all spotted a hideous creature
400 yards away from the ship. They were able to clearly see the
monster with binoculars. The creature was seen just before sunset
and lingered for just a 5 minutes.
The creature appeared to race the ship as times and had a neck
15ft. Long and a jaw of about a foot wide. It swam in an
undulating motion before disappearing under the water.

Sept 1894
The Captains of the steamer ships George F. Williams and H.A.
Hawgood both stated that they saw a massive sea monster
between Whitefish point and Copper harbor.

The Great Squid of Duluth

 Summer 1897
Duluth, Minnesota
 A sailing crew from the Detroit yachtsmen club reported being
attacked by a giant-squid monster. They were bowling along
through 10ft of water when they struck a rock. One of the men in
the confusion fell over board and was sucked underneath the
water by an undertow.
The man saw a gleam of two eyes in the dark water and then he
felt a sickening sponginess around his waist. He began fighting
for his life and was able to push off the lake bottom. The creature
kept tightening it's coils around him. The water was a pinkish
foam all around him for 10 to 15 ft. He believed the creature was
75ft long and dark green in color with great scales and it had a
forked tail.

1930's
Pictured rocks, Lake Superior.
 Two fishermen saw an unknown sea creature. It looked to see
snake shaped and moved as 8 to 9 miles per hour.

Pressie of Lake Superior

Lake Superior's resident lake monster. Described as serpentine
and dark in color. Pressie has a horse-like head and a whales tail.
It has whiskers and measures 75 feet in length.

Memorial Weekend 1978
Ironwood, Michigan
A hiker saw two dark humps in the water, A few feet apart. He
noticed that the humps would submerge and then raise up out of
the water. He then noticed a 3rd hump in the water and soon
realized that the creature was undulating through the water. It
quickly swan through the water and left a noticeable wake in the
water.
 He stated it was as wide as a Volkswagen and resembled an
anaconda.

Chapter Seven

Lake Monster Hoax's and Fakes.

In the late 1990's the remains of a Burbot fish became the famous remains of sometimes called the "Erie Baby," the approximately 3 feet long carcass had reportedly washed up on the shore of Lake Erie around 1992, at which time it was found and then stuffed by taxidermist Mr. Larry "Pete" Petersen, who displayed it at his "L & D Bait and Tackle" shop near Cleveland, Ohio until Mr.Carl Baugh bought it from him.

At some point after Mr. Petersen had stuffed the Lake Erie monster baby, Mr. Carl Baugh of Texas got word of the creature. Mr. Baugh then traveled from Texas to Petersen's shop to examine it. During his visit Mr. Baugh purchased the specimen from Mr. Petersen and then put the creature's body on displayed at his Creation Evidence Museum in Glen Rose, Texas. Mr. Baugh evidently accepted the oddity as a real, plesiosaur-like lake monster.

Around the same time strict creationist Mr. Kent Hovind began to promote the creature in a similar manner in his seminars. A photograph of the stuffed creature appeared on his website, where he had stated the following:

"In 1998, I talked to Pete Peterson who lives in
Cleveland, Ohio. He said he was walking on the beach
about six years earlier and found a dead baby
creature three feet long. The seagulls had been
pecking at it. Pete took it home with him and
mounted it. He's a taxidermist. He said this creature
was lying on the beach of Lake Erie. Strange looking
little fellow. Four flippers and has a tail
sort of like a fish. He said it had something like
pouches on the side of its cheeks. Carl Baugh bought
it and it's in the museum in Glen Rose, Texas now.
They've done a DNA analysis and a CAT scan x-ray. It
had a fish hook stuck up in its head. Apparently
somebody caught it sometime in the past and broke the
line. The fish hook is still in there, it shows up on
the CAT scan. Strange little critter."
        (Mr.Hovind, 2002-2006)

In an interview with Mr. Glen J. Kuban, Mr. Petersen explained
finding the Baby monster and Mr. Petersen was surprisingly
candid about the manner in which he had processed the carcass.
Mr. Petersen said that when he found it, it was already decaying
and had been "pecked at" by birds, but was evidently some kind
of fish, with a hook still in its mouth.

Mr. Petersen stated that he decided to stuff it and fashion it into a
sea-serpent like creature as an attention-getting display for an
upcoming taxidermy trade show. Mr. Petersen said it had a long
fin along the rear part of the body, which he notched into
triangular shapes to make it appear more dragon like. He also bent
and sewed the neck into an S-shape to foster the same impression,
and finally, sewed little pieces of skin to form little flippers.

 Mr. Petersen said that the display, which was basically a "joke"
was a hit, and that many people at the trade show enjoyed it,
especially children. He said he did not think anyone would take it
seriously, until Mr. Baugh showed up and seemed to assume it
was a real lake monster, and wanted to buy it. Despite being a
taxidermist, Petersen said that he was unable to identify it.

Mr. Kuban concluded that it was almost certainly a long-bodied, somewhat eel-like fish called a burbot, whose scientific name is *Lota lota*, and which can grow to 36 inches or more in length. Also known as an eelpout, ling, lingcod, and lawyer fish (among other names), it is one of the few fresh-water relatives of ocean cod, and is less common than most Lake Erie species (usually preferring deeper, cooler waters), but is known to exist in Lake Erie.

Mr. Hovind states that DNA analysis and a CAT scan was conducted on the specimen, but does not provide the results. However, in 2005 Mr. Kuban discussed the specimen with Mr. David Woetzel, whose own web site once encouraged the idea that the creature was some kind of lake monster. Mr. Kuban related to Woetezel his research and findings, indicating that the creature was indeed an altered long-bodied fish. Soon afterward Mr. Woetzel related that he had discussed the matter with Mr.Baugh, who told him that he had also concluded that the creature was some kind of "eel."
To Mr. Woetzel's credit, he soon removed the section of his website regarding the creature. Evidently Mr. Baugh himself no longer promotes the carcass as a baby lake monster, nor have any other major creationist groups

In 2007 Mr. Carl Baugh posted an update on his Erie Baby (which he now calls "Baby Erie") in the FAQs section of his <u>Creation Evidence Museum website.</u> In an apparent attempt to distance himself from his initial suggestions that the carcass represented a young plesiosaur, Mr.Baugh wrote that a "science teacher" (evidently referring to Mr. Kent Hovind) suggested that it had the appearance of a juvenile plesiosaur but that the presence of a dorsal fin and lack of heavy flippers were "not plesiosaurian."

Mr. Baugh relates that his "staff" ran the specimen through a medical CAT scan and that the vertebrate and associated bones were deemed missing. He surmised that evidently these bones had been removed by the taxidermist. Mr. Baugh did not say why he could not learn more from the skull that remained.

Mr. Baugh claimed that he took the x-rays and specimen to the head of a "Marine Biology Department" at a "major state university" who was excited about the specimen, suggesting it was a "throwback" to early marine evolution. However, Mr. Baugh did not reveal the name of the biologist or the name of the university.

Nor was he willing to reveal the name of another "marine biology department" head that he had subsequently showed the specimen to. This department leader was reportedly unable to give any identification of the creatures species. Mr. Baugh then claims that a "credentialed microbiologist" (again, no name mentioned) from a "third major university" (also unspecified) reported that the taxidermist's acid had destroyed any DNA in the specimen, but believe the specimen was an unclassified eel. That it was deserving of technical publication.

If that account was even accurate. It seems rather surprising that neither Mr. Baugh or the biologists he visited bothered to compare the specimen's head with known fish from the Great Lakes, which would have readily revealed that it was a modified burbot fish.

Instead, Mr. Baugh seems to leave the impression that the carcass represents an exotic prehistoric "throwback" unknown to science. Further fostering this impression, Mr. Baugh recounts being referred to a "reliable individual" who reported seeing a creature identical (except larger) in "a lake in southern Canada." However, if this account is true, one must wonder why Mr. Baugh again refrains from naming the individual involved or even the name or specific location of the lake.

One must also wonder, if Mr. Baugh really wanted to know or share the whole truth about this specimen, why he seemed reluctant to conduct further research. He relates that the Canadian witness invited him to spend a few weeks at the lake searching for the mystery creature.

The carcass that was once advocated by Mr. Carl Baugh and Mr. Kent Hovind as a probable "baby lake monster" from Lake Erie and by Mr. Baugh to be an unclassified exotic eel, is evidently merely the altered remains of a long-bodied fish known as a burbot as Mr. Petersen had originally stated.

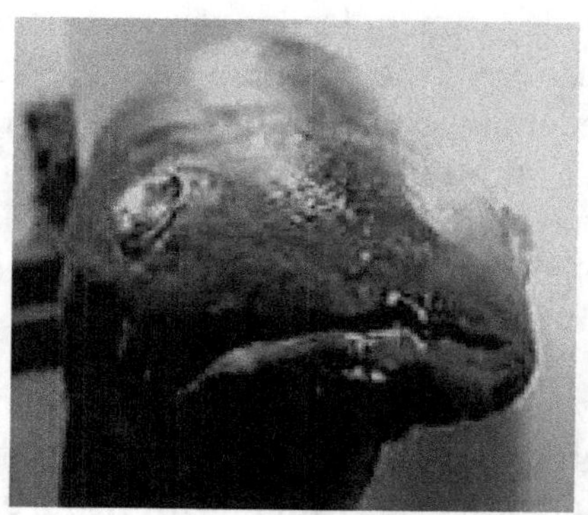

Live burbot

Lake Ontario monster hoax

 The monster KINGSTIE was part of a hoax in 1934. It scared
two fisher man as is floated passed on empty bottles with it's fake
dragon head.

Chapter Eight

Water monsters of inland lakes and water ways of the Great Lakes.

Michigan's Inland water monsters

Stearn's bayou Monster

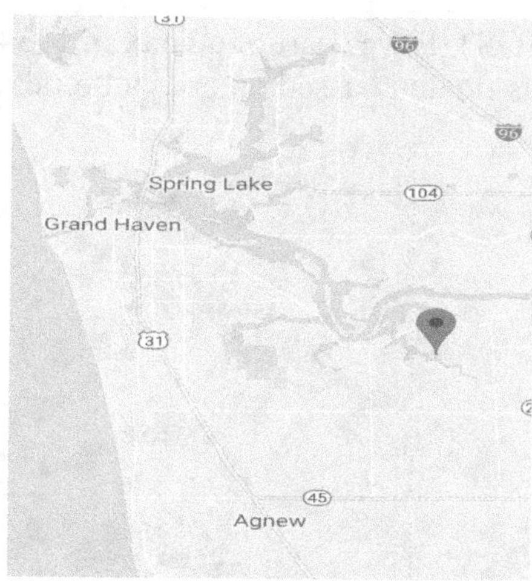

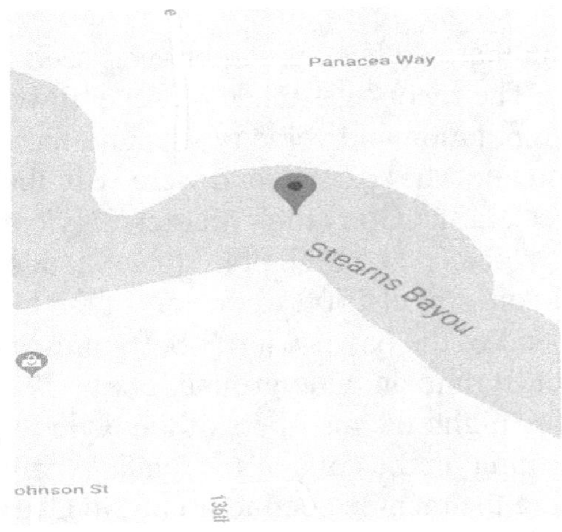
Panacea Way
Stearns Bayou
ohnson St
136th

information from an article published in the Grave Haven Tribune on August 13, 1909

A report came in that another sea serpent was seen in the water of Stearn's Bayou. The report was made by several well known citizens whose reputation and veracity was unimpeachable. Dr. Chase W. Cotton and Mr. H.Z. Nyland were with their families spending the week at the Gun club's quarters, Nylcott camp.
 The cottage was located at a high point that extends out into the waters of the bayou. About 150ft to the left of the highway bridge. At the head of the bay is Clark's bottomless pond which may be an outlet from to an underground lake.
Late that Monday night, the members of the Nylcott party were enjoying the evening on the cottage's veranda. At around 9:30 p.m. That evening the men decided to go to Sid Clark school for an ice cream social. During the men's absence the ladies heard strange noises coming from the vicinity of the bridge.
They claimed the noise resembled the sound of about 200 large sheephead drumming. With tremendous groaning and barking like some ferocious beast in anger and distress.
The sound appeared to get closer to the cottage and the ladies made a retreat into the cottage. The creature passed by the front of the cottage and out into the bay with a sound of great gulping.
One of the ladies reported seeing a streak of light along the surface of the water but they were all to frighten to further inspect outside.
Upon returning the men claimed that the ladies were just hearing noises and let their imaginations go wild.
A Mr and Mrs. Chas B. Shupe were also staying with the Nylcotts that weekend when the creature returned. The men ran outside to investigate and saw a hideous looking beast moving through the water. It had a head like a Hippopotamus, a 6 feet in diameter soft shelled turtle's body and a tail of about 10 feet. It emitted a phosphorescent light from under itself. The creature swam up the bay and sank below the water's surface.

The party quickly added rifles to the camp and organized a group of other campers and farmers to help catch the creature. They did not catch the creature.

A hippopotamus type head was reported for the monster

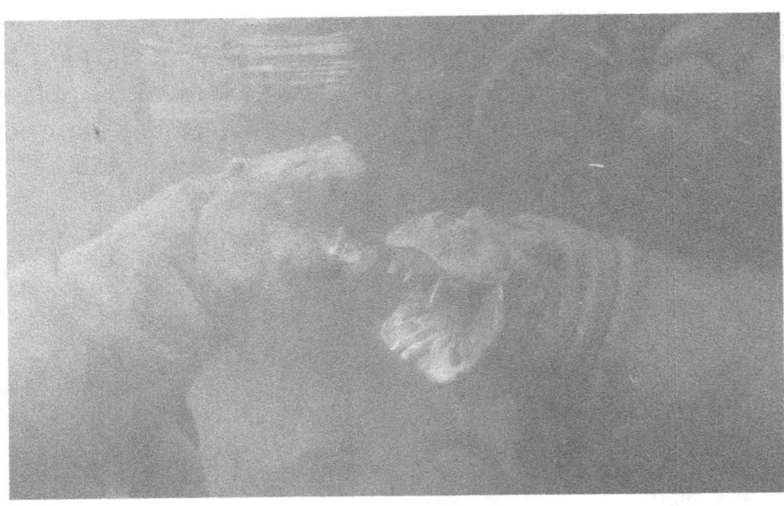

August 20, 1909

Mr. Geo. E. McCabe and family went up to spend the weekend at the gun club's cottage on Stearn's bayou. They arrived at the cottage at 6:30pm and had supper. They prepared to retire for the evening at 10:00pm. After trying in vain to fall asleep for several hours, Mr. McCabe arose and went outside to relax.

The night was beautiful and a soft breeze blew across the bayou. As Mr. Mac relaxed and rested outside he became aware that a dark shape was plowing across the surface of the lake.

The creature had a dim phosphorescent glow and the outline of a monster turtle like creature could be seen.

It had an elephantine head and a long serpentine neck. A crocodile like tail could be seen.

It moved with giant flippers and was moving as fast as a motor boat. Mr. McCabe watched as the creature made it's way onto land and with a rush came onto the beach in front of the cottage. Mr. McCabe watched as the creature moved up the beach and dug a hole with it's front flippers. It made a purring sound and a grunting like a disturbed hog.

After an hour the creature made it's way back into the water and left behind a partially filled hole. It made a roaring sound as it entered the water and then slipped beneath the water.

Upon searching the area where the creature had dug the hole. A perfectly round egg was found. It was Described as being yellow with red spots. The size of a large pumpkin and feeling like thick leather.

The McCabe and Nylcott party were very upset and took the egg into the city to have it seen by authorities but upon returning home the egg fell overboard and was lost.

The egg was never recovered.

The Lake Leelanau monster

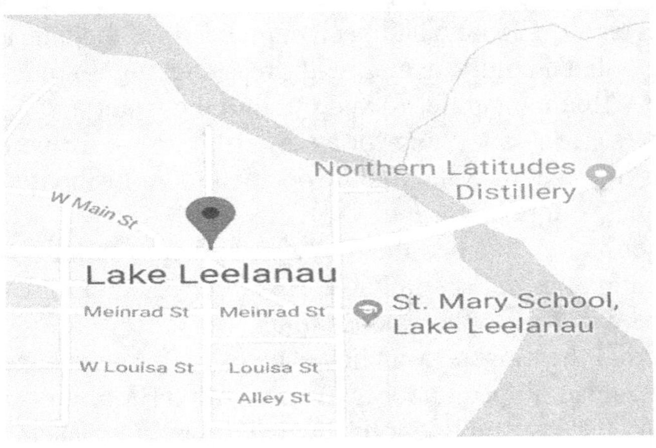

1910 Lake Leelanau

 A boy was fishing for perch one day in 1910 in the shallows of
Lake Leelanau. The lake had been damned since the late 1800's
and resembled a boggy swamp with trees sticking up in it.
The boy William Gauthier rowed out into the water and up to one
of the trees. He was looking for a new fishing spot for perch. His
boat was in 7 feet of water and he decided to tie his boat to the
tree and cast out his first line.
No sooner had he touched the tree with his rope, then two eyes
were staring at him. Face to Face. This tree was sticking 5 feet up
out of the water and was 6 inches thick.
The boy and the monster watched each other for several seconds
before the head dipped under the water with a Blooping sound
and the monster swam under his boat. The creature's head pass the
front of the boat and it's body was longer than the boy's boat. It
swam away in an undulating motion.

Michigan's other lake monster homes

Au Train Lake- a large fish circles boat 1870s

Basswood Lake-

Carter Lake-Giant Black snake

Deweie Lake monster- Aquatic Bigfoot sightings and attcks

Lake Charlevoix- Sturgeon

Narrow Lake?

Paint River-swimming moose

St Mary's River?

Straits of Mackinac-Mishpeshi

Swan Lake- swimming cow.

Torch Lake monster

Thunder Bay- Water panther

Trout Bay, Lake Superior- (Small Whale)

Williams Lake-possible big fish?

Illinois inland lake monsters home

Lake Decatur Giant Catfish

Lake du Quoin & Stump Pond-Giant Catfish

Four Lakes Village Quarry, Lisle-Giant Catfish or Giant
Salamander

Indiana inland water monsters

Lake Manitou Monster

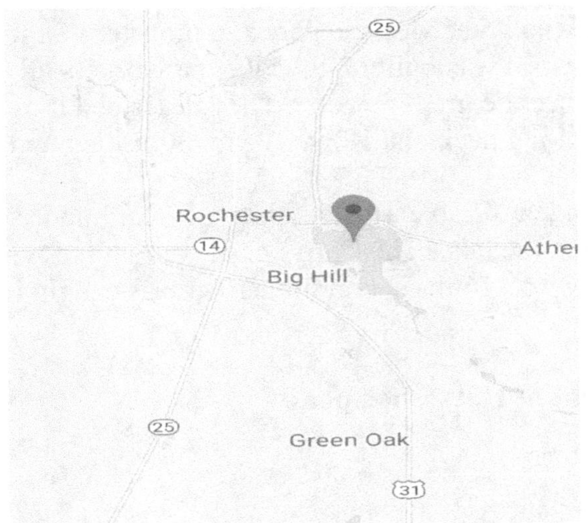

   The potowtomi tribe forbid any of their peoples to hunt near the Manitou lake or fish in it's waters. They warned the white settlers who came and formed the town of Rochester not to use the lake either.
They feared the great Meshekenabek, a monster that lived in the lake. After a mill was built on the lake the workers all started claiming to see the great monster. They described it as a serpent's body with a long neck and Horses head. 30 ft long and dark in colors.
In 1849 a huge buffalo carp weighing "several hundred pounds" was caught in the lake. The Carp's head was said to weigh about 30lbs. In 1889 a 116 lbs spoonbill catfish was caught in the lake.

The Serpent of Horseshoe pond

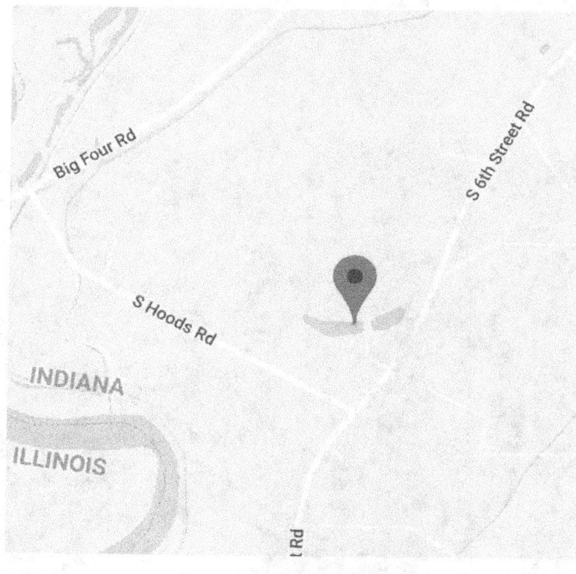

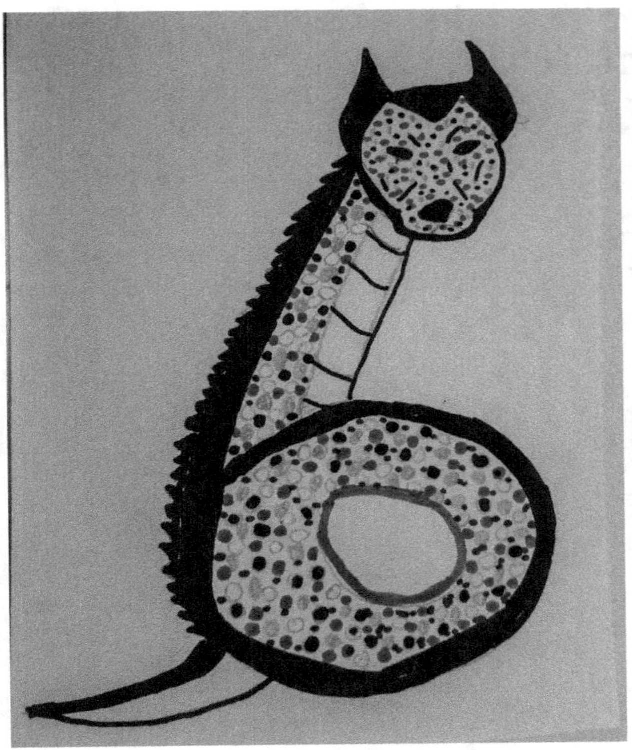

 Horseshoe pond is located 6 smiles south of Vincennes, Indiana.
 The Serpent that called that pond home was said to be 60ft longer
and bigger than a telephone pole. It looked like a snake but had a
dog-like head.
One witness a Mr. Issav Daines reported his sighting to the
Vinennes commercial on April 22, 1892. The newspaper
described Mr. Daines as a respectable local farmer. He claimed
the following." Its color was black on the back and sides. It
inhibits the water and does not seem to venture any distance on
shore, It glides through the water of the pond with that easy and
graceful movement peculiar to a snake swimming. When
approached it becomes alarmed and swims away.
The creature has a white throat and belly, with mottling on it's
sides of red and yellow.

Oscar, The beast of Churubasco

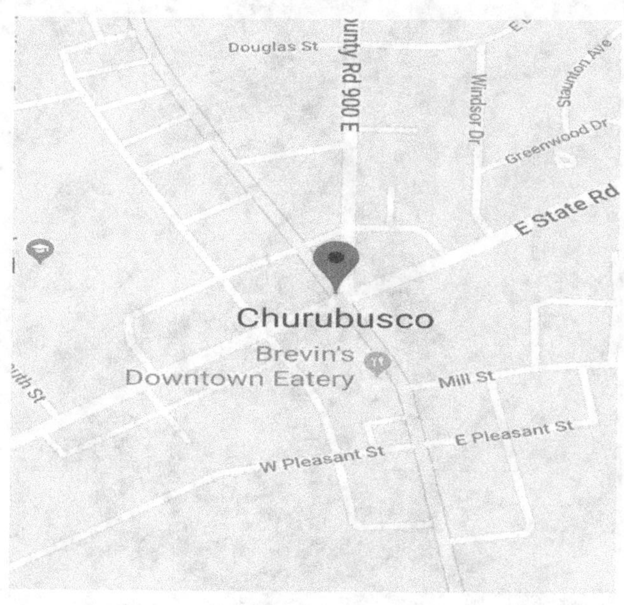

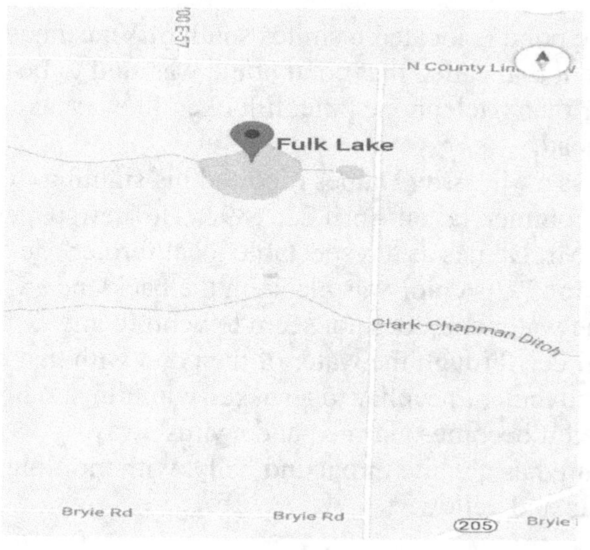

Oscar as he was named by Oscar Fulk was described as a gigantic snapping turtle. He was 5 feet wide and lived in Fulk lake on the Fulak farm. Fulk lake is a 7 acre located east of the town of Churubasoc.
 The Fulk farm became the epicenter for many tourist looking to see the giant turtle. First in 1898 when he was first sighted and then 50 yrs. Later in 1947 when he was once again spotted in Gale Harris. This time the turtle made national news and everyone was out to find the turtle who was now the size of a dinner table and maybe 400lbs.
"The Beast of Busco" has a become the towns claim to fame now. Every year in June there is a parade and turtle days festival.

Green Clawed beast/Ohio river monster

 Mrs. Darwin Johnson was allegedly attacked by an unseen monster while swimming in the Ohio river. On August 14, 1955 Mrs. Darwin Johnson and her friends were traveling to their swimming spot in Evansville, Indiana when they spotted an UFO They paid no attention to it and continued on their way.
 Mrs. Darwin said while swimming that a hairy clawed hand grabbed her leg and pulled her under the water.
It was able to drag her under the water twice before she was able to escape. Once she reached land, she discovered a green palm stain on her leg.

Indiana other lake monster homes

Bass Lake-Giant Catfish

Big Chapman Lake Warsaw-Giant Beaver

Big Swan Pond, near Vincinnes-Giant Beaver

Eagle Creek?

Hollow Block Lake, near Portland-Giant Beave

Lake Maxinkuckee

Wabash River-Giant Beaver, slaps tail on water

White River-Giant Catfish

Ohio inland water monsters

 On January 11, 1878, Ben Karrick spotted a sea serpent near the Roebling suspension bridge in the Ohio river. He described the serpent as protruding from the water about 12 to 15 feet. It was moving quickly through the water and lashing the water into a foam with it's tail.

The creature made a hissing sound followed by a deep lowing that sounded like a cow. It's head looked to be covered by black, glossy hair and an alligator like hide. It's head appeared to be sea horse-like.

The local Gazette announced that a similar creature had been spotted years before near the Clermont county Hartman mill damn. That serpent was reported to be 15 to 20 feet long.

Another creature was by spotted by Captain John Davidson on the Silver moon steamboat, he described the serpent as swimming like a Sea lion, it had a long pelican beak, slimy mane and was extremely long.

On October 23, 1879 an Alligator was caught in Cincinnati on the river. A Surgeon named A. Jackson Howe took possession of the alligator.

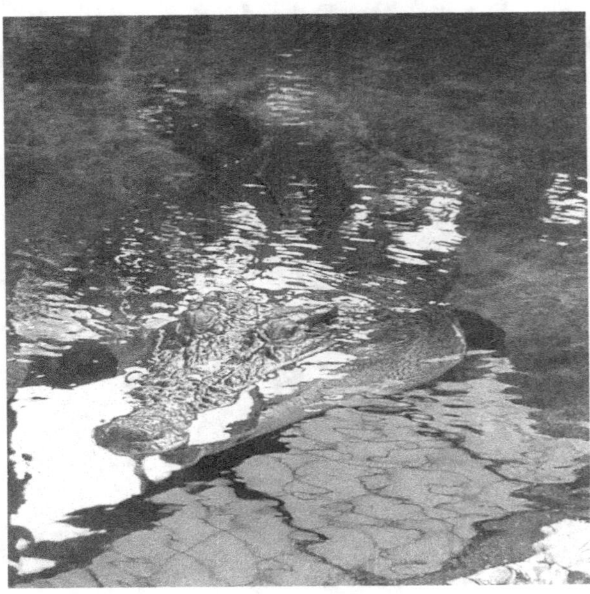

Loveland frogmen

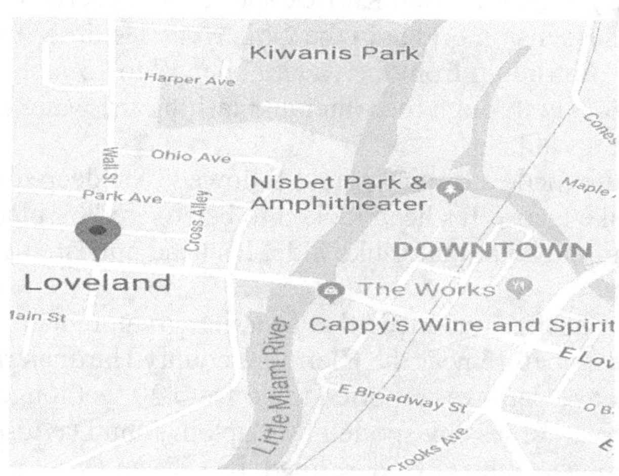

In May 1955, Loveland, Ohio became home to a group of strange creatures. A traveling salesman saw 3 creatures huddled together on the side of the road in the early morning hours.
The Creatures had leathery green skin, webbed hands and feet. They had frog-like faces and one seem to be creating sparks from a stick it was holding.

Crosswicks Monster

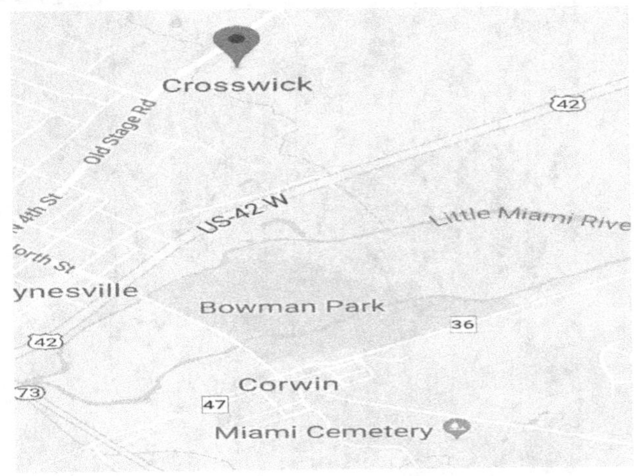

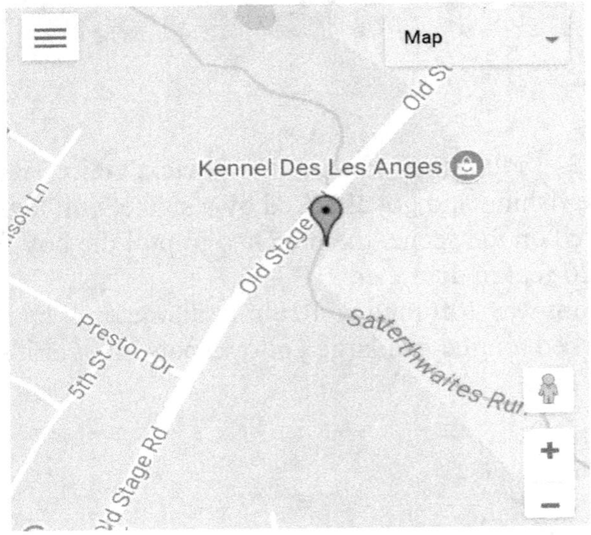

 May 1882, In the small town of Crosswick, Ohio. Two young boys were fishing and got attacked by a snake with legs. When help arrived on the scene, the men had to pull the boy from a tree that was 26 feet in diameter.
The creature was 30ft long and 16in in diameter. It had 4 long legs, a forked tongue and large yellow spots all over it's scales.

Ohio's other Lake monster homes

Cuyahoga Valley-Peninsula Python-Giant Blacksnake

Ohio River-Giant Blacksnakes and Giant Salamanders

Olentangy River-Giant Beaver hippo-sized

Slaven's Pond Bridge-Giant Salamander

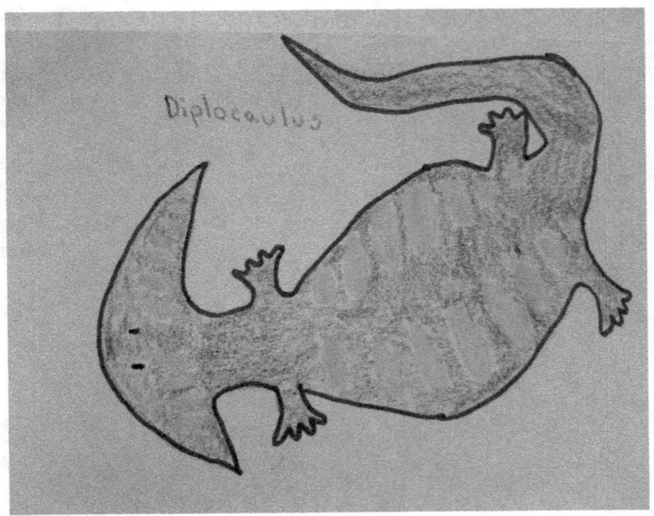

Minnesota inland lake monsters

Lake Pepin

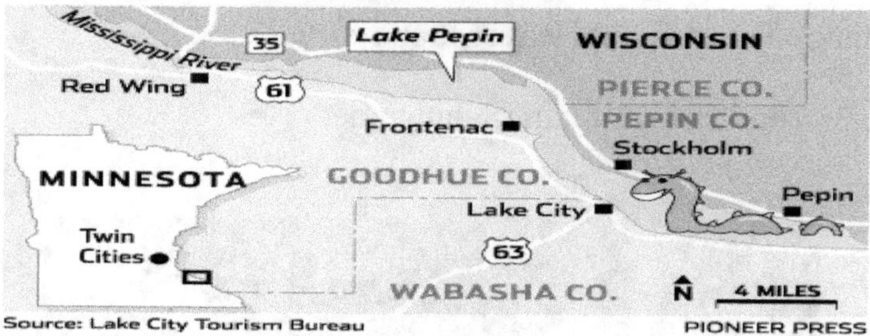

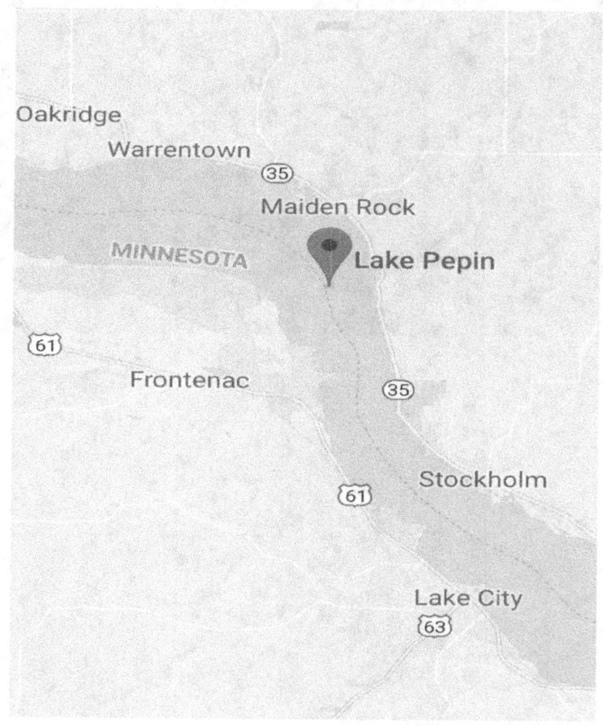

  Pepie has been sighted in the Lake Pepie area since the 1600's. Modern sightings include water skiers and boat captians. While some photographs have been taken of a blurry object in the lakes waters. No true credible photos have been taken.
Many expeditions have been launched in hopes to find and document Pepie but none have been successful. Descriptions range from a plesiosaurus to snake-like.

Minnesota's other possible lake monster homes

Basswood Lake-Waterspout

Big Pine Lake-Oscar-Giant Sturgeon

Big Sandy Lake-swimming moose

Leech Lake-Possible Giant Sturgeon (2) detected on sonar 1976

Minnesota River-Hoax

Lake Minnetonka- unidentified wave action with unknown cause

Wisconsin inland water monsters

The Devil's lake Monster

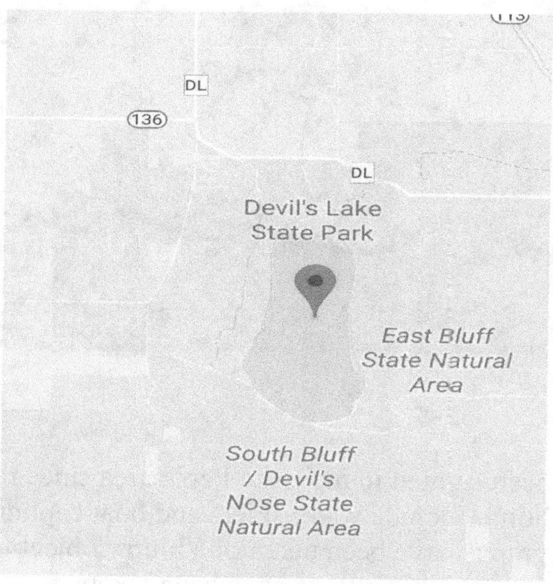

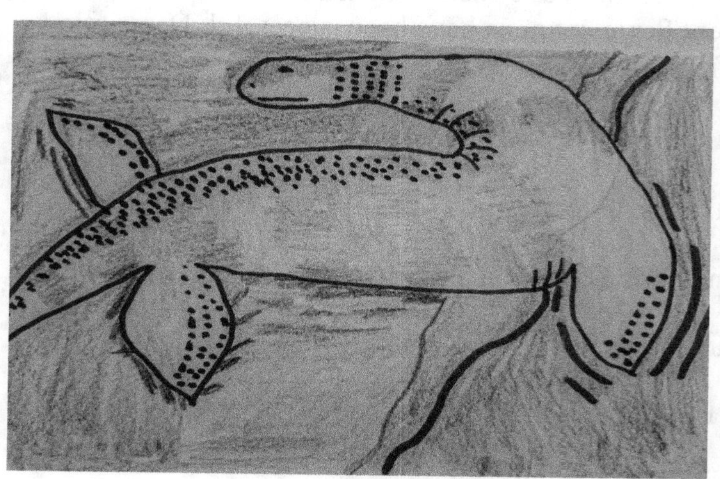

Devil's lake was called Da-wa-kah-char-gra by the Ho-chunk
tribe. The spirit lake was known for it's voices of the dead that
could be heard during celebration.
The Nakota tribe had a legend about a water monster they called
Unktizina that they witnessed being stranded in the drying lake.
The creature was seen wiggling itself back and forth between the
waters as it was stuck in the mud. The creature finally freed it's
self and swam away.
The creature was huge with a long neck and small head.

Another monster of Devil's lake was the freshwater Octopus that
was known for attacking Native hunting parties and canoes.
It's interesting that Devil's lake is a cold deep salt-infested lake.
The legend goes that A Native Chief sent a hunting party across
the lake and once the canoe was half way to the other side of the
lake, A flurry of tentacles came out of the water and capsized the
canoe. The terrified men were pulled beneath the water.

Bozho, the lake Mendota monster

Bozho was name after an Ojibwe folk hero named Winnebozho. The curious creature is know for tickling sun bathers feet and overturning canoes. One witness described the creature as looking like a pliosaur, a type of plesiosaur. It has a snake-like head and a mischievous grin.

Rock Lake

89
94
W Madison St
N Main St
Mulb
Lake Mills
E L
89
89
Bean
Lake State
Natural Area
Topel St
A

The Great protector of the underwater pyramids of Rock lake. The pyramids some say were built by the Aztalan tribe. Rocky is a large serpentine reptile. He is said to dwell among the deepest sections of the lake. Rocky is said to be very violent to boaters.

Lake Monona

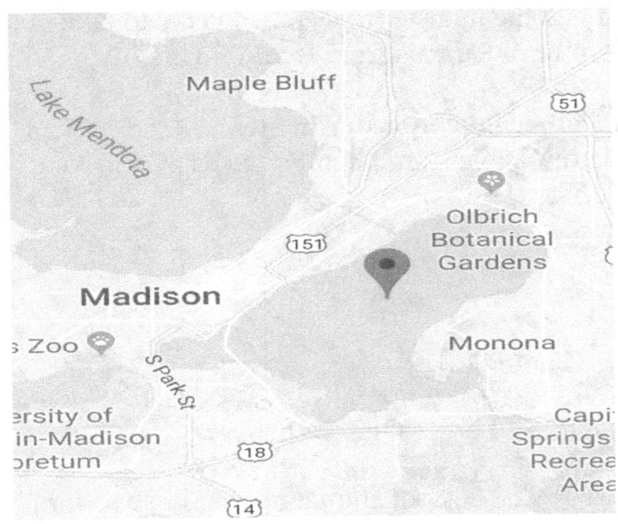

The Lake Monona monster was reported to be 20 feet in length. Dark green in color and traveled with it's head held in a snake-like manner above the the waters surface. Some witnesses claim it also had flashing eyes and spouted streams of water.
It would feast on swimming dogs and pigs that came close to shore to drink.
It's rumored that the monster moved from lake to lake in the area and ate lots of farm animals from local farmers.

Wisconsin's other lake monster homes
Browns Lake-probable sturgeon reported as 27 feet long and with barbels as "Huge teeth"
Chippewa Lake

Devlan Lake

Elkart Lake- Giant Pike

Fowler Lake-1892- Large "Otter or Beaver"

Lake Geneva-1892-100-foot animal reported to overturn boats-likely a wave action

Lake Kegonsa

Keshina-Mythical

Koshnkonong Lake-Giant Pike

Lac La Belle Immense Fish

Mississippi River Mythical

Oconomowoc Lake

Okauchee Lake 6-foot long Pike

Pewaukee Lake

Red Cedar Lake- Sturgeons

Lake Ripley unidentified wave action

Sturgeon Bay, Lake Michigan-Giant Sturgeon or Water Panther or Giant Otter

Lake Waubesa-Giant Sturgeon

Lake Wingra-Snapping Turtle

Lake Winnebago-Giant Sturgeon

Yellow River

Chapter Nine

Waves and their tricks.

If you sit on the beach and watch the waves of any lake for long enough You will see anomalies in the tide.
Depending on the wind speed, rain, storms or passing boats. The water reacts to whatever it comes in contact with. A wind swept wave becomes a dark surge rolling across the horizon. A floating log or piece of drift wood becomes animated in a storms aftermath.
From a mile away these waves can look like animals or sea serpents.

From the deck of a ship or canoe, These can look like a great sea serpent.

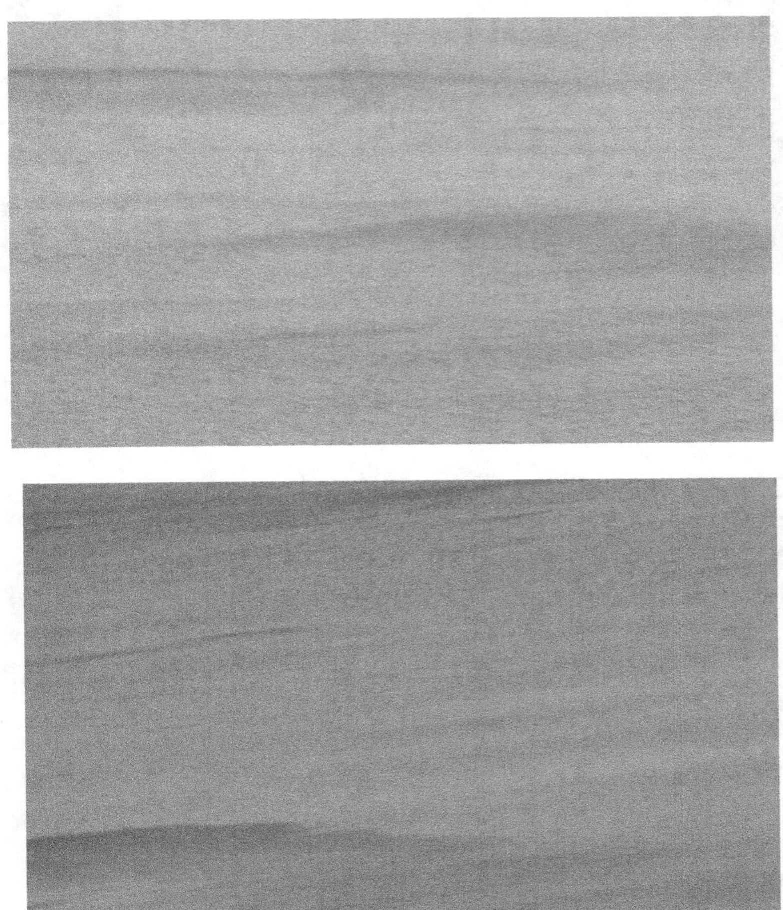

Bibliography

Internet

http://paleo.cc/paluxy/eriebaby.htm

http://frontiersofzoology.blogspot.com/2011/10/giant-catfishes-and-other-lake-monsters.html?m=1

http://www.therapidian.org/prehistoric-michigan-covered-ancient-seas-tropical-jungles

http://www.livescience.com/29312-great-lakes.html

http://www.fossilguy.com/gallery/vert/fish-shark/shark_evolution/shark_evolution.html

https://blog.nationalgeographic.org/2012/08/17/freshwater-sharks-species-of-the-week/

https://www.sharksider.com/sharks-of-the-arctic/

http://www.sharksavers.org/en/education/biology/how-bull-sharks-survive-in-fresh-water/

http://www.wideopenspaces.com/18-waters-u-s-canada-reported-mystery-lake-monsters/

http://mysteriousuniverse.org/2017/04/exploring-american-monsters-wisconsin/
http://www.phantomsandmonsters.com/2013/08/lake-monsters-inwisconsin.html?m=1

http://hauntedohiobooks.com/news/mystery-reptiles-mysterious-beasts-part-4/

http://mysteriousuniverse.org/2015/10/exploring-american-monsters-michigan/

http://michigansotherside.com/the-stearns-bayou-water-monster/

http://www.cryptopia.us/site/2010/10/devils-lake-monsters-wisconsin-usa/

http://atthecreation.com/wis.monsters/deep.html

http://www.strangemag.com/strangemag/strange21/unnaturalindiana/unnaturalindiana5lakemonst.html

https://en.wikipedia.org/wiki/Beast_of_Busco

http://www.cryptopia.us/site/2010/01/bessie-usa-canada/

http://cryptidz.wikia.com/wiki/Lake_Ontario_Serpents
http://cryptidz.wikia.com/wiki/Bessie

http://www.northernontario.travel/algoma-country/the-lake-superior-dragon-and-other-stories-of-great-lakes-monsters

http://www.chroniclet.com/news/2015/05/24/Prehistoric-fish-discovered-in-Lake-Erie-debuts-on-Animal-Planet-show.html

http://web.ncf.ca/bz050/HomePage.glm.html

http://www.cryptopia.us/site/2011/06/leelanau-lake-monster-michigan-usa/
http://articles.latimes.com/1990-09-30/news/mn-2507_1_lake-erie

http://cryptomundo.com/bigfoot-report/pressie-the-lake-superior-monster/

http://seamonster.org/

http://www.native-languages.org/morelegends/oniare.htm

http://www.native-languages.org/lake-monsters.htm

https://retrieverman.net/tag/bull-shark-lake-michigan/

http://www.denvermichaels.net/

http://markturnersmysteriousworld.blogspot.com/2011/05/great-lakes-mystries-monsters-ghost.html?m=1

Books
Stonehouse, Frederick. Haunted lake huron, lake myths, wrecks and spirits. Lake superior Port cities Inc. Duluth, Mn 2007

Stonehouse, Frederick. Haunted Lakes, Great lakes ghost stories, superstitions and Sea serpents. Lake Superior Port cites Inc. Duluth, MN 1997

Stonehouse, Frederick, Haunted Lakes 2, More Great Lakes Ghost stories, Lake Superior port cities Inc. Duluth, MN 2000

Butts, Ed. Shipwrecks, Monsters and Mysteries of the Great Lakes. Tundra books CANADA 2010

Mayo, Willam and Barthel Kate. The Mysterious North shore, a collection of short stories about Ghosts, UFO's, Shipwrecks and more. Adventure publications, Inc. Cambridge, MN 2007

Lewis, Chad and Voss, Noah. Pepie the lake monster of the Mississippi river. On the road publications. Eau Claire, WI. 2014

Michaels, Denver, People are seeing something, A survey of lake monster in the United states and Canada. 2016

Holman, Alan J. In quest of Great Lakes Ice age vertbrates, Michigan state university press. East Lansing, Michigan 2001